NUMEROLOGY:

The Language of Life

Ruth Drayer

ISBN 0-944132-12-X

Published by Skidmore-Roth Publishing
207 Cincinnati Avenue
El Paso, Texas 79902
1-800-825-3150

Printed in the United States of America

Dedicated to
my dear friend and teacher,
John-Roger

Acknowledgements

The suggestion that it was time to write this book came while I was in New York City from Keith Critchlow, world authority on Sacred Geometry. Undoubtedly he was right, as it has flowed through my fingers with a life of its own. Writing it has been a great blessing and joy for me. Many dear friends, loved ones, and "well-wishers" have shared in my process, and to them I owe great thanks and appreciation.

I wish especially to thank Elizabeth Moore and her family, Mary, Rebecca and Margaret, for being "my family." Also, Patrice Ridgeway, Helga Carrion, and Richard Powell for sheltering me; Grace Giles for healing me; Christine Carter Lynch for always being on the other end of the line; Jean Hocking for typing and holding my hand, so to speak; Mrs. Birdie Sheridan at the Atlantic County Historical Society for helping research Mrs. Balliett; Mark Hochwender for holding the light; my children and their spouses for enriching my life. Greatest appreciation and heartfelt thanks go to my Guardian Angels for the superb job they do.

Las Cruces, New Mexico

Contents

Acknowledgements / *v*

Introduction
The Fairy Tale / 1
History of Numerology,
   The Science of Name and Number / 3
      Pythagoras / 5
      Mrs. L. Dow Balliett / 10

Chapter One
Constructing the Chart / 13
      General Ideas and Information / 24
      Free Will / 26
      Importance of the Name / 28
      Importance of the Birthday / 29

Chapter Two
A Complete Introduction to the Numbers / 37
The Odd Numbers / 39
      1 / 40
      3 / 45
      5 / 50
      7 / 56
      9 / 62
The Even Numbers / 71
      2 / 72
      4 / 77
      6 / 83
      8 / 90
      0 / 97

The Master Numbers / 99
    11/2 / 101
    22/4 / 102
    33/6 / 103
    44/8 / 104

Chapter Three

Speaking the Language / 107
    The Inclusion Table / 107
    Planes of Expression / 114
    Name Changes / 122
    More on Birthdays / 124
    An Advanced Look at the
    Pinnacles and Challenges / 124
    Personal Cycles / 126
    Personal Years / 127
The Table of Events / 135
    Constructing the Gameboard / 135
    Universal Cycles / 138
    How to Read a Chart / 141

Bibliography / 155

I'm going to tell you a fairy tale...

The Fairy Tale

Once upon a time, long ago, when a baby was born upon the earth, it had total knowledge of its spiritual heritage and complete remembrance of its past lives. It knew why it was on the planet and what it needed to learn here. Then a witch waved her magic wand over the babies and put forth a spell that said, "From this time hence, most babies will be born in total innocence with no recall of the past and no knowledge of the future. All such information will be stored through a code and carried around as their name and birthday. To decipher this code, they will have to become students of the ancient sciences such as Numerology, the study of vibration: names, numbers, colors, and sounds (and Astrology, but that's another story)."

And so it happened that way.

And for a long time people heard the word "Numerology" and had no idea what it meant. Still, the study endured and trickled down with the sands of time until about the year 1972 A.D., when lo and behold, books started springing up everywhere talking about hidden things and mystical paths and extrasensory experiences. And all of a sudden, someone looked at the numbers and the alphabet and said, "Hmmmm. There must be more to this than meets the eye.... I think I'll dig around and see what I can find out about these strange little symbols that look so innocent but show up everywhere around me constantly." The symbols looked like this: 1 2 3 4 5 6 7 8 9 0. So they started looking in old bookstores and libraries and studying hidden tomes and cobweb-coated pamphlets. Soon they had a smidgen of the truth stored there and said, "Can it really be that life has a purpose and meaning and that I have lived lots of times before?" The more they meditated on these questions, the more they knew and understood and the more joy and peace they had in their lives. Soon they were ready to share their knowledge with others, and started writing books and articles, and teaching classes, and giving private readings (to decipher the code for those who didn't know how).

Most of what they learned led them to conclude that people are not really victims of the universe, but rather co-creators, with power and control over their lives. And the more understanding they could have of themselves, the easier and more harmonious their lives would flow. And further, that the study of Numerology and the other occult (which means hidden) sciences leads to a broader view of what life is really about. Also, they learned to observe with less emotion and involvement the everyday soap operas through which each family lives.

And so, dear readers, that is why your name is so special and why your birthday is such an important and, I hope, happy time of celebration for you (and why people who say they are "too old" for birthdays are missing out on something special), and why the reason baby-namings are such special, joyous occasions. These are all constant reminders to us that we are very special, unique beings here on Planet Earth, and we're very lucky to be here.

◪

ॠ

Ⴀhe Science of Name and Number

Ⴀhe challenge of writing about Numerology is in finding the perfect words to assist in a process whose goal is to open the intuition and allow what is there to unfold. Yet Numerology is the perfect tool for doing this, as it speaks a language structured exactly for this purpose. "By means of this language it is possible to identify areas of reality normally beyond investigation, to extend logic into the realm of intuition, and to activate parts of the mind otherwise dormant" (John Michell, *City of Revelation* 1972). In other words, we are dealing with a centuries-old method for integrating and balancing both hemispheres of the brain for the purpose of bringing greater harmony and balance to each person involved.

Throughout time, people have been looking for the laws that would bring order and harmony to their lives; sifting through, analyzing rules of grace, proportions, relationships in music, architecture, art, agriculture, mathematics, geometry; hoping that a thorough knowledge of the outer world would assist in "man knowing himself." Numerology studies the outer world *and* the inner world, all the laws being the same.

The study of Numerology gives the ability to isolate each trait and characteristic, see its inherent balance or imbalance, and bring it into a more harmonious whole. It gives symbols to the voices that speak inside us.

"The esoteric, functional aspect of Number, for instance, would be apprehended through the 'right hemisphere' faculty, while the exoteric, enumerative aspect of Number is apprehended by the 'left'. This innate intellectual quality resembles very closely what the Greeks called 'Pure Reason', or what in India was called the 'Heart-Mind'. The ancient Egyptians had a beautiful name for it, the 'Intelligence of the Heart', and to achieve this quality of understanding was life's implicit goal." (S.K. Henninger, Jr., 1974)

"According to Theon of Smyrna, the Pythagoreans viewed numbers as the source of form and energy in the world…dynamic and active even among themselves…almost human in their capacity for mutual influence in that they can be androgynous or sexual, procreators or progeny, active or passive, heterogeneous or promiscuous, generous or miserly, undefined or individualized. They have their attractions, repulsions, families, friends; they make marriage contracts. In fact, they are the very elements of nature. These tools of geometry represent the means to attain knowledge of both external and internal space and time. These instruments, once used by architects and philosophers, became, during the Age of Reason, the tools of the engineer" (Robert Lawlor, *Sacred Geometry, Philosophy and Practice*, 1982).

Numbers not only have a life of their own, they fully and completely represent all of our lives. Wonderfully intricate plots of fiction could be woven solely from the interactions of their characteristics. Are we just numbers, or are numbers just us?

To study Numerology is to study light, color, sound, and form, as they are all vibrations. To understand our own vibrations is to understand how to heal, balance, and transform ourselves into our most perfect self; love and acceptance are the tools necessary to appreciate our own special uniqueness. That appreciation then is reflected in rhythm, beauty, grace, and joy.

What the witch took away with a wave of her magic wand was the knowledge of ourselves as individual expressions of God's unlimited creativity. In our confusion, we tried to be each other. This book is devoted to reminding us that we are children of joy, light, color and sound, not carbon copies of each other. We are unique beings, dancing the dance of life with our own intricate steps.

To assist you in using my words as a basis for opening up your own natural knowing, please try to "feel" as you "read." That way, you may get a fuller meaning of what I am attempting to convey. Words can be so expansive and so limiting, all at the same time. Please expand what I am saying by using your imagination to include more.

Along with the words, I have come up with several techniques for you to use in order to participate more actively. These take the form of questions and little play assignments. As you use them, you will be including more of your sensory skills. Be assured there is no right or wrong. Your intuition is *always right* — even if it appears different from another's.

Pythagoras

About 600 B.C., there lived in Greece a truly amazing man named Pythagoras who sought to discover and be able to demonstrate the unity of all things. He saw the "triple nature of man and the universe, penetrated by God" reflected in architecture and everywhere he looked. He felt the key to the universe was concealed in the science of numbers, and observed "the worlds moving through space in accordance with the rhythm and harmony of the sacred numbers." (Edouard Shure, *Pythagoras*, 1923) Imagine this: he spent the first fifty-four years of his life studying (in Egypt, Persia, and all the great centers of learning) before returning to Greece and starting to teach. He is credited with being the Father of Numerical Analysis, now called Numerology.

In my beginning days of studying Numerology, I was aware that Pythagoras was credited as the Father of Numerology and so was intrigued to learn more about him. It was a particular point of interest to me as I'd had trouble understanding high school math, and the only thing that I'd really retained from those years was Pythagoras' name on a theorem. So I started researching him, and the more I've read about him the more in awe I've become. It amused me to read somewhere that an author wondered if such a person could ever have existed at all. Being credited with so many achievements, he might have been like Paul Bunyon, with tales that grew bigger and bigger as time passed by. This author went on to say maybe there was just a school named "Pythagorean." Pythagoras' students were famous for quoting the master so copiously that for centuries they were recognized by the words, "The master said it...."

It's written that before his birth, the oracles of Delphi told his parents Pythagoras would be descended from divinity to become a very noble and important person, useful to all men throughout all time. And so to prepare, they went to a sacred isle for his conception and consecrated him in utero, to the worship of Apollo. Another version claimed his was a virgin birth, as was commonly expected of an avatar and great teacher in those days (600 B.C.).

The most distinguished priests and masters were his teachers, and by age twenty he had studied in all the centers of Greece and found much contradiction among them. He wanted to find a path leading to the sun of truth, to the center of life. During a night of great confusion, as he was trying to sift through the truths of his teachings, he looked above to the infinite heavenly bodies and awoke to the knowledge that while each world has its own law, still all move together according to number in supreme harmony. In a flash of illumination, he saw mankind living in three worlds: the natural, the human, and the divine. With this understanding, he came face to face with the realization that although there could be numerous gods and countless teachings, there is only one divine God, the essence and spirit in everything.

Pythagoras knew he must now prove by reason what his intellect had learned from Divine Intelligence. He flashed back to the blessing received as a child from a priest at the Temple of Adonai, which said while the Greeks possessed the science of the gods, the knowledge of God was only to be found in Egypt. He realized that he needed this "science of God" to penetrate to the very heart of nature. He resolved to go to Egypt and undergo initiation. This decision started a search that continued for the next thirty-six years, until he proved his theory of the trinity of the universe, man, and God.

It is said that he journeyed earlier, farther, and assimilated more knowledge than any other eminent philosopher. In all his travels he studied with the elite of each country, passing through the initiations necessary for admission to the priesthoods and sacred schools of learning. Pythagoras felt each school taught a portion of the universal truth, and his goal was to synthesize them into one body of knowledge. He learned the virtues of numbers and geometry in Egypt and the effects of the planets from the Chaldeans; he spent time with the Phoenicians, the Persians, the Hindus, the Arabians, the Jews, the Orphics, the Druids, touching every center of learning in the world of his day.

Finally, at age fifty-six, he returned home to settle in Croton, Italy, and founded a secret society open to both women and men. His society for initiates was the prototype for all later philosophical schools, including those of Plato and Aristotle, who were the ninth and tenth in line to receive his teachings. The regulations of the school were very strict and severe, with students attending their first five years in silence. The initiated were sworn to the utmost secrecy. While everything pertaining to human knowledge was covered in the school, it's impossible to go to any one document (or even a few documents) for a thorough explanation of his philosophical system. It is said that, without exaggeration, his teaching has touched every major classical philosopher, scientist, and church father—including Galileo, Copernicus, and Kepler. During the Renaissance, his teachings permeated almost every learning and discipline. He and his students were all vegetarians, and his dietary laws included abstaining from alcohol and beans.

Pythagoras' society held out to its members the hope of divine perfection, with numbers as the means of rising above the everyday world. Each student was dedicated to the release of his soul through purification and meditation. Experience of God, through the study of nature, was the ultimate goal. Instruction was offered which began with mathematics, proceeded to physics and the investigation of primary principles, and finally promised knowledge of God. He was attempting to teach realization of God through scientific study rather than religious rapture. These secret teachings were the beginning of the systematic study of the physical sciences, of astronomy, mathematics, geometry, and music. (Perhaps if they had explained to me in school that the purpose of geometry was to measure heaven, I would have done better!) Pythagoras offered a mode of thought that kept people firmly in this world, yet faced in the direction of the next. Underlying each of these disciplines was Pythagoras' theory of numbers. The Pythagoreans were the first to apply themselves to mathematics and studied numbers as the principles of everything, saying: they could see in numbers both the beginnings of the universe and the ultimate things in the universe; that the elements of numbers were the elements of everything, and that the whole universe was a proportion or number.

The Pythagoreans' beliefs touched every field of human endeavor: ethics, theology, science, politics, art, architecture, and the applied arts such as geography, navigation, and astrology. Pythagoras figured out the principle of musical octaves and intervals, invented many words such as "philosopher" and "kosmos," and discovered the law of opposites. He was the first to compose a book on the properties of plants. He had a reputation as a seer in touch with spirits, a necromancer who could control them, an interpreter of dreams, a sorcerer, an alchemist, an astrologer, and a master of the magical lore of all nations. The Wheel of Fortune survives from the time when Pythagoras designed it as a fortune-telling device.

Pythagoras is described as tall, in good physical condition, fair to look upon, solemn and dignified, clothed in white with a crown of gold around his head. He is said to have had a "golden thigh, visible proof of his near divinity" in addition to his incredible intelligence. To him were attributed many supra-human powers: he could converse with animals, fly, and appear in two places at once. Because of his purity, he alone of all men was able to hear the Music of the Spheres, the ever-present harmony in heaven — music that the planets and the stars make as they traverse the heavens. (Reportedly, music generated by each planet contributing a note to the harmony of heaven that plays continually; we could only hear it if it stopped.) According to the Pythagoreans, this harmony is latent in our innermost being, allowing us to participate in the larger harmony of the universe and endowing our lives with music, concord, and joy. They believed our senses of sight and hearing were for the purpose of regulating our own internal harmony with the harmonious motions of the heavenly bodies.

Pythagoreans believed in "the plurality of worlds," the existence of other worlds comparable to earth which were inhabited by creatures more or less recognizable to us; they believed the moon and every star was a world by itself, containing earth, air, and sky in an infinite celestial nature. He taught of a spherical earth that traveled in a circular orbit around the sun and of people with immortal souls subjected to reward and punishment through reincarnation (he could remember all of his own). According to Plutarch, Pythagoras explained that an eclipse of the moon was due to the interpolation of the earth between it and the sun.

In Renaissance France, several academies were based explicitly on Pythagorean assumptions about numbers and harmony. In the book *Gulliver's Travels*, loved by generations of children, Gulliver found in Lapata, a full-blown Pythagorean society completely devoted to mathematics, astronomy, and music.

In the opinion of a classical scholar in 1706, "If the glory of a philosopher is measured by the duration of his doctrine and the extent of the places that embraced it, nothing can equal Pythagoras since most of his opinions, to this day, are followed by the greatest part of the whole world. Greece's two most excellent men, Socrates and Plato, completely followed his doctrine and methods of explanation," and are frequently quoted in our time, centuries later. (S.K. Henniger, Jr. *Touches of Sweet Harmony*, 1974)

Pythagoras, along with many of his followers, was persecuted and assassinated, and all of his schools and libraries were burned around 495 B.C. He was seventy-five at the time. Credit him with these accomplishments, and with influencing minds for two thousand years through a set of beliefs that touched every area of human life. In the Pythagorean scheme, religion and science not only coexisted, they were mutually dependent. To the Pythagoreans, the cosmos was the source of beauty, the mold for beauty, and the standard by which beauty was recognized. It was a world integrated harmoniously to hearing the sounds of God.

Somewhere around the time of Sir Isaac Newton (1642-1727), life got complicated enough in commerce and science that new demands were put upon the numbers. They became practical things to be used in the daily affairs of men. At the same time, as if it all went underground, there was a great springing up of secret societies and mystical literature hidden from the eyes of the everyday world.

While it can be amply substantiated that Pythagoras learned Numerology in Egypt and taught it to the Western world, I've read both that the Hebrews gave this sacred study to Egypt, and also that the Hebrews learned it while they sojourned in Egypt. There is also evidence that the science of numbers was used by the Chaldeans over 11,000 years ago. It was also studied by the Phoenicians, the Hindu in India, Chinese, Tibetans, in Arab countries, among the Mayans, the American Indians and the Magyars.

Mrs. L. Dow Balliett

In 1847, an astonishing woman named Sarah Joanna Dennis was born. A student of the Bible as well as the works of Pythagoras, Plato, and other philosophers, she originated Western Numerology, calling it The Balliett System of Number Vibration. Her book, *The Philosophy of Numbers*, was published in 1908 and several others followed, all written under her married name: Mrs. L. Dow Balliett. Her books are very spiritual and focus on awakening people to the knowledge of themselves as Divine Beings through color, sound, and vibration. She spoke liberally of reincarnation and how choice affects our lives. In 1911, she was principal of the School of Psychology and Physical Culture in Atlantic City, New Jersey. She writes of traveling overnight by train and actually hearing *The Music of the Spheres,* describing it as "faint, glorious music that arose from the depths of earth and sea, silvery, watery, fiery, and the unity of the whole so blended that it filled me with awe." She was a speaker with The New Age Thought Church and School and became friends with its founder, Julia Seton Sears, M.D., who is credited with modernizing the name into Numerology. Dr. Seton authored a book herself in 1912, *Your Aura and Your Keynote* (Physical Culture, Atlantic City, New Jersey). Her fourteen-year-old daughter, Juno Belle Kapp, studied with Mrs. Balliett, and later went on to make most of the modern contributions that have brought Numerology into being the useful study that I am now presenting. Dr. Juno founded the California Institute of Numerical Research to study numbers. It existed for 25 years and *Numerology, the Romance in Your Name* was published with their findings. I've looked upon it as my main reference. The Planes of Expression, the Challenges, Pinnacles, and the Table of Events started through the Institute's work. Their book presented their views in such a positive light that it allowed Numerology to come alive for me and many others throughout the world. Mrs. Balliett died in 1929 at the age of 82, and Dr. Juno Jordan passed over in 1984, two months before the age of 100. I call them the Mothers of Numerology, and extend to them my great love, devotion, and appreciation for their impact on my life, and now, perhaps, on yours....

࣠

BIRTH DATE
SIMPLIFIED

ADVANCED

= ◯ BIRTHPATH

AGES:

CHALLENGES

PINNACLES

ATTAINMENT:

HEART'S DESIRE
DESTINY
PERSONALITY

PLANES OF EXPRESSION:

MENTAL: EMOTION:

PHYSICAL: INTUITION:

INCLUSION
TABLE

1.
2.
3.
4.
5.
6.
7.
8.
9.

TABLE OF EVENTS

AGE	1	2	3	4	5	6	7	8	9	10	11	12	13	14	15	16	17	18	19	20	21	22	23	24	25	26	27	28	29	30	31	32	33	34	35	36	37	38	39	40	41	42	43	44	45	46	47	48	49	50
19																																																		

ESSENCE

PER YEAR

CHALLENGE

PINNACLE

CHAPTER ONE

Constructing
the Chart

This book is about the joy to be found through the study of numbers. It is about the light, color, and sound of vibration. This is about you—and what you vibrate to. This is about the "Music of the Spheres" of which Pythagoras spoke. We are the music of the spheres—the old esoteric truth: as above, so below—as the planets and stars sing to us, so also do we sing to them! This is a book of musical notes, a how-to book on orchestration (of our lives), encouraging all to put their whole heart into singing and making "a joyful noise unto the Lord".

Now, with a wave of *my* magic wand, it's time to break the spell that was cast and unlock the mystery!

So the first step in Numerology is: *Construct the Chart.*

A chart is the very heart of a Numerology reading. It needs to be done slowly and with great care and attention. One little mistake can throw off all your calculations and turn your name—or birthday—into someone else's. Several charts have been included so that you can do yours as we go along, and for others you are interested in charting. (The more you do, the easier it gets.)

AMELIA   MARY   EARHART   PUTNAM

7 5 9 1   8 9 1 7   5 1 7   3 4 1

4 3   4 9   98 92   7 25 4
7   4   1   9

BIRTH DATE JULY 24 1898

SIMPLIFIED   ADVANCED

○ = ○ BIRTHPATH

AGES:
0 - 33
33 - 42
42 - 51
51 —

CHALLENGES   PINNACLES

HEART'S DESIRE (4) (9)
(7) (8)
DESTINY 3 8
PERSONALITY

PLANES OF EXPRESSION:

MENTAL: 6   EMOTION: 2
PHYSICAL: 4   INTUITION: 5

ATTAINMENT: 1

INCLUSION TABLE

1. 5
2. — 1
3. — 1
4. — 2
5. — 2
6. — 1
7. — 1
8. — 1
9. 4
  17

TABLE OF EVENTS

AGE	1	2	3	4	5	6	7	8	9	10	11	12	13	14	15	16	17	18	19	20	21	22	23	24	25	26	27	28	29	30	31	32	33	34	35	36	37	38	39	40	41	42	43	44	45	46	47	48	49	50
1898	99	00	01	02	03	04	05	06	07	08	09	10	11	12	13	14	15	16	17	18	19	20	21	22	23	24	25	26	27	28	29	30	31	32	33	34	35	36	37											
	A	M	M	M	E	E	E	E	L	L	L	L	R	R	R	Y	Y	Y	Y	Y	M	M	M	A	A	M	M	M	E	E	E	E	L	L	L	L	Y	Y	Y	Y										
	M	M	M	A	R	R	R	R	R	R	R	R	R	R	Q	Y	Y	Y	Y	M	M	M	A	R	R	R	R	R	R	R	R	R	R	R	T	T	E	E	E	E										
	E	E	E	E	A	R	R	R	Q	Q	Q	Q	Q	R	R	H	H	H	H	H	H	H	R	R	R	R	R	R	R	R	T	T	E	E	E	E														
ESSENCE	10	13	13	10	15	13	13	23	21	21	21	21	27	25	24	24	24	24	24	13	6	17	14	6	22	22	23	23	23	23	23	14	15	21	21	21														
PER YEAR	3	4	5	6	7	8	9	1	2	3	4	5	6	7	8	9	1	2	3	4	5	6	7	8	9	1	2	3	4	5	6	7	8	9	1	2	3	4	5	6										
CHALLENGE	1																														1	2																		
PINNACLE	4																														4	5																		

The information on the chart is actually divided into thirds: the Name; the Birthday; the Personal Cycles and TABLE OF EVENTS (which pulls together all the threads and weaves them into your own personal tapestry). This chart will become your friend and tell you secrets that will be simple as you begin, and deepen as you advance. (I have been doing Numerology for about fifteen years at this point, and it truly amazes me that new and more subtle information continues to come forward — just from this little chart, and my intuition.)

While your chart is being constructed, you'll already be on your way to learning Numerology. As the letters of your name are coded into digits, or your birthday unravels its mysteries, turn to Chapter 2 and read what each number symbolizes so that you start to feel it from every angle. Although they have different slants and dimensions, basically A NUMBER MEANS THE SAME WHEREVER YOU MEET IT, so once you become familiar with a digit, anywhere it shows up you'll already have a relationship with it.

If you can pretend this is your first exposure to these little symbols, 1, 2, 3, 4, 5, 6, 7, 8, and 9, it might assist you to open more of your own intuition. And to "jog" your unconscious a little, they're being presented in an unusual form: all the "odd" numbers together, and all the "evens" together. Please remember this big key to simplify things: NUMBERS MEAN THE SAME WHEREVER YOU MEET THEM — and I may say it one more time to make sure you "get it."

In Numerology, we primarily work with the single digits 1 through 9, and compounded numbers 11, 22, 33, and 44. Any digit larger than 9 is REDUCED down by adding all the digits together.

Example: 1989 reduces to 9 by adding
$1 + 9 + 8 + 9 = 27; 2 + 7 = 9.$

If a sum has a 0 at the end (20, 30, 40, etc.), simply drop the 0 to have the reduced digit. 11, 22, 33, and 44 are treated as if they WERE reduced and as if they WEREN'T, and so are written 11/2, 22/4, 33/6, and 44/8.

So, we'll start with THE NAME, and now it's your turn.

HEART'S DESIRE ♡ ♡
DESTINY
PERSONALITY ☐ ☐

INCLUSION
TABLE

1.
2.
3.
4.
5.
6.
7.
8.
9.

PLANES OF EXPRESSION:

MENTAL: EMOTION:

PHYSICAL: INTUITION:

Fill in your FULL name as it appears on your BIRTH CERTI-FICATE. (Use this name even if you have never used it—whether you like your name, or not—this is still the first step.)

1	2	3	4	5	6	7	8	9
A	B	C	D	E	F	G	H	I
J	K	L	M	N	O	P	Q	R
S	T	U	V	W	X	Y	Z	

Step 1. Give every VOWEL its number. (Y is considered a vowel if there is no other vowel in the syllable.)

Step 2. Now add the VOWELS, first of each name separately and then *reduce*, and secondly all names together and then *reduce*. Fill in the little heart with the *reduced* total amount of all vowels. This is called THE HEART'S DESIRE, and symbolizes the very heart of your name. It literally represents where your heart lies—or is the happiest. It has also been termed the "soul urge," as it represents the soul or essence of the name.

Step 3. Give every CONSONANT its number.

HEART'S DESIRE ④ ⑨   INCLUSION

DESTINY   ⑦ ⑧   TABLE

PERSONALITY   ③ ⑧

1. **5**
2. **1**
3. **1**
4. **2**
5. **2**
6. **-**
7. **1**
8. **1**
9. **4**

17

PLANES OF EXPRESSION:

MENTAL: **6**   EMOTION: **2**

PHYSICAL: **4**   INTUITION: **5**

Step 4. Add the CONSONANTS of each name separately, and *reduce,* and then add them all together, and *reduce.* Fill in the little square with the total. This is called the PERSONALITY, and symbolizes the outer self or what your name projects to the world. It is not an accurate description of you—simply as you appear. If the HEART'S DESIRE and PERSONALITY are the same—it is a fortunate occurrence and represents a special harmony inside you.

Step 5. Add all the numbers of each name, *reduce,* and fill in the little circle above it. Add together all three names (or however many you have), *reduce,* and fill in the waiting circle. This is called THE DESTINY, and symbolizes all your past lifetime accomplishments and the energy patterns you are working with now. It represents who you are and what strengths you have to sustain and empower you. It is what you are here to do.

PLEASE NOTE: The tendency now will be to add the vowels to the consonants to arrive at the full total of each name; however, if there is a mistake in the addition, you will miss it. To check your addition, the full name needs to equal the SUM of the VOWELS plus CONSONANTS.

Step 6. Fill in the INCLUSION TABLE by counting HOW MANY of EACH NUMBER is in your name. DO NOT REDUCE HERE. This table explains the energies you have developed through past lives—now brought with you as gifts, talents, and general tendencies. We will read it for both the HIGHEST amount, and which (if any) numbers are MISSING. The highest amount represents great strength, while missing numbers represent out-of-balance areas— weaknesses or undeveloped traits. Missing numbers are generally referred to as "karmic numbers."

Step 7. Count the amount of letters in your name. It needs to equal the *total amount* of numbers in the Inclusion Table.

Step 8. Constructing the PLANES OF EXPRESSION: do NOT reduce here. From the INCLUSION CHART, *total* the amount of 1's plus 8's present in your name and fill in the line of the MENTAL PLANE. *Total* the 4's plus 5's and fill in the PHYSICAL PLANE. *Total* the 2's, 3's, plus 6's and fill in the EMOTIONAL PLANE; remaining are 7's and 9's—fill in INTUITIONAL PLANE.

PLANES OF EXPRESSION are a detailed study that provides an incredibly valuable source of information about the manner in which a person thinks = Mental Plane; acts = Physical Plane; feels = Emotional Plane; and senses = Intuitional Plane. The Planes can reveal the inner conflicts a person can experience and are a significant contribution in relationship compatabilities. You may want to save this part of the chart until you are comfortable to go on to a little more advanced Numerology.

Step 9. If you are not presently using your Birth Name, follow the above procedure and fill in your name as you THINK of yourself. This is called your present signature. Names at birth are our foundation. Frequently, it was that name that got us to the point where we could change it for something else. It continues to exert its influence, even if it was never used. If you've had several names over the years, use the Birth Name and only your present one.

Pause and review — how much do you remember?

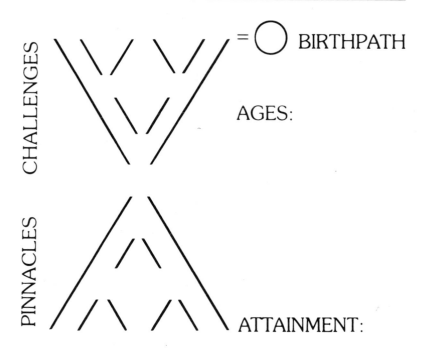

On to THE BIRTHDAY. Birthdays are important enough to have complete studies of Numerology built around them. They can be relied on when you feel uncomfortable with the accuracy of the Name numbers you've charted; as, for instance, in reading the name of someone who was originally named from an alphabet such as Hindi, Chinese, or Arabic. There will be times when the birthday information substantiates the name, and others when it will greatly enhance and supplement it—explaining things that are difficult to comprehend.

Step 10. Using January as 1, February as 2, March as 3, etc., REDUCE your month, day, and year of birth.

Step 11. Total those three digits and reduce, and fill in your BIRTHPATH. It is your major lesson in life and something we work to master—we have from birth 'til death to accomplish this. Compare it to your "major" in college.

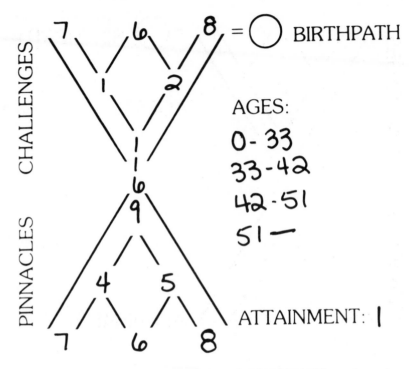

Infrequently, the DESTINY and BIRTHPATH total to the same digit. This indicates a great emphasis on this quality and assures you of doing whatever it symbolizes. So as your life progresses, your approach and understanding would shift and grow. During your span of years, your interpretation of what it means may vary and swing around until eventually you become expert in understanding that quality. It is believed this configuration may indicate an unresolved issue from past lifetimes, and so you're bound to "get it" this time around.

Step 12. The CHALLENGES and PINNACLES are four phases in the development of the BIRTHPATH and can be compared to the other classes necessary to graduate. They represent the abundant study and research necessary to getting a liberal education here on Planet Earth. The timetable is individually structured and determined by your BIRTHPATH. To find yours, subtract your BIRTHPATH from 36 (36 is considered the cycle of mankind).

Amelia's Timetable:

36 (Cycle of Mankind)
- 3 Amelia's Birthpath
33

Birth (0) till 33 years
33 till 42
42 till 51
51 for the rest of her life

(a) The length of the first cycle extends from birth (age 0) until the age EQUAL to the SUBTRACTED SUM.

(b) The second cycle is 9 years in duration.

(c) The third cycle is 9 years in duration.

(d) The fourth cycle starts where the third ends and indicates you've completed your prescribed course of study and are ready to go out into the world and use your education.

Steps 13 and 14 will be devoted to finding the PINNACLES and CHALLENGES. The concept of them and how they work can be a little difficult in the beginning, as it requires us to look at our life in a very different perspective. It necessitates our separating things in our minds which are not usually separated which can be as difficult as explaining the step-by-step procedure of what happens with your feet when you walk. That might take a little thought.

The CHALLENGES and PINNACLES are valuable for giving a clearer understanding of what we're doing in life, and can be viewed as the name of the subject or class you're taking at that period of your life. PINNACLES are a state of mind: our attitude or viewpoint. CHALLENGES teach on a more physical level. For instance: Your house catches on fire. What could you learn from that? You could learn that you have the strength to rebuild or that you were far-sighted enough to have adequate insurance. Perhaps you'd discover friendly neighbors that could be depended upon in an emergency; many things can be learned from each experience. CHALLENGES operate more on the outer level, PINNACLES on the inner. It seems to me that the CHALLENGES actually "challenge" us to grow in a certain direction, and the PINNACLES ask us to demonstrate what we've learned. Another way to look at them is that CHALLENGES are the experiential portion and PINNACLES are the theory. For example: In a 5 *Challenge* (as a first challenge), a young person will frequently have parents who move a lot, service people for instance, or perhaps they're divorced and the child goes back and forth between them. In a 5 *Pinnacle*, however, the child may not even move its little physical body but is usually thinking about running away or reading travel and escape books and plotting what he will do when he is "free," something you can bet will be Bohemian or out of step with other people. The 5 definitely marches to the tune of its own drummer and wants freedom at any cost.

Another example: With a 1 *Challenge* (as a first challenge), the youngster is alone a lot and has to rely on himself—for instance, being put up for adoption, left alone without parents or friends—even the dog runs away; every time he tries to lean on someone, that's not allowed. With a 1 for a first *Pinnacle*, the child is a leader: the captain of the team demonstrating great courage and wanting things to go his way.

Because of the length of the first cycle, it establishes the foundation upon which the life is built. It happens that some people then try to hold onto this period for the rest of their lives, wondering what has gone wrong with them that they are not doing the things they were so sure would always be important and significant. A good example of this would be someone who put lots of time and money into preparing for a career under one Challenge and then no longer is interested in it upon entering the next. Imagine the ramifications of such an action—not only inside themselves, but feedback they get from their friends and family. And yet, life really is change, and trying to hold onto the first Challenge is as realistic as fighting hard to stay in the fifth grade all your life!

So the first Pinnacle and Challenge, for most people, is a significant, long period of their lives, followed by *two cycles* each of nine years, and finally into the *fourth* cycle in which they put to use all the knowledge and wisdom they've developed.

Upon entry into the fourth and last Pinnacle and Challenge, another number comes into prominence. It is called the "ATTAIN-MENT" and is the synthesis of the full Name at birth with the Birthday — the coming together of the two most important forces, Numerologically speaking. At the time people start thinking about retiring, they've actually just arrived at the time they have been working towards all those years.

One of the mindsets most of us accepted early in life was that there is "something" out there that we're supposed to be doing, if we can find "it." When we do find "it," we do "it" until we retire. Maybe that starts with the childhood question, "What are you going to do when you grow up?" As a result, some people try to hold back from being more adventurous and in tune with themselves. Through the Challenges and Pinnacles it's obvious that moving from job to job can be a normal flow or progression. Maybe it's true that "you can't teach an old dog new tricks," but people are not really dogs, and challenge and growth is what we are about on Planet Earth. Living life fully is always finding new problems to solve, new experiences to experience.

Step 13. PINNACLES are found by adding the DIGITS of your BIRTHPATH — they're added UP. Try it out on your chart.

Step 14. CHALLENGES are found by subtracting the DIGITS of the BIRTHPATH — they're subtracted DOWN. Fill it in slowly.

To Repeat: The length of the first cycle is determined by subtracting the Birthpath from 36. The next two cycles each last nine years. The fourth cycle begins when the third ends, and extends its influence until death.

For Amelia:

$$36$$
$$-\ 3$$

Birth to 33

33 years until 42 and
42 years until 51
51 years —

For this we got complicated, as both subtraction and addition were needed. The subtracted portion is called Challenges. The added portion is called Pinnacles. They go hand-in-hand and operate on the same time schedule. They are read *from left to right*.

Pinnacles are added and go UP; Challenges are subtracted and go DOWN. Reduce each step as you go along.

Pinnacles
1. Add the month plus the day
2. Add day plus year
3. *Add* the *total* from Step 1 plus Step 2 = 3
4. Add the month plus the year = 4

Month	Day	Year		Month	Day	Year
July	24	1898	=	7	6	8

Challenges
1. Subtract month from day
2. Subtract day from year
3. *Subtract those answers* from each other
4. Subtract the month and the year

(Please subtract whichever number is smaller from whichever is greater.)

General Iõeas anõ Information

In the beginning, people commonly have a strong desire to rush through the beginning pages to "get to the good stuff," yet I encourage you to take your time passing through and thoroughly familiarize yourself with the next few pages. You are preparing to learn an ancient art or science for opening your intuition with symbols that are timeless and ageless as well as a completely new language and philosophy.

I suggest to you that the teaching that will be going on through the vehicle of these pages by way of written words, is on many different levels and so needs to be taken slowly. Please utilize all the games and suggestions offered for immersing yourself in this study.

The more you put into it, the more you will receive from it. Ancient teachings were transmitted orally, because once an idea is put into written words, it limits a person's perspective. Most of us tend to take someone else's word as the authority instead of checking inside ourself for our own perception. While centuries of written words have been extremely beneficial, we've come to the time where we are again unlocking our natural knowing. One of my goals is to assist you to reawaken in yourself a tiny place that has been slumbering, waiting for this very moment.

The form of this book is unique in that everything that belongs together about each number is in one place so that you can get a real feeling for the characteristics or personality of that symbol. When you're finished, you'll have a good general understanding to depend upon yourself and you'll be able to draw upon your own intuition.

There is a common myth that we "have one number" or "are one number." I want to explode that myth. We are intricately complicated beings who could never be explained by one symbol, number, or vibration. In all the years I've been doing Numerology, I've never found two people with completely the same numbers.

While Numerology actually lays out the full blueprint of a person's life, there is no way to completely predict the choices a person will make, or ascertain if they are living their life in a positive style or a negative one.

To know and be able to read a complete name and birthday is to have knowledge of that person, in this life, and others past. There is a great responsibility that goes along with this information: literally, to revere each as a unique child of God, one only, a soul that deserves great respect, love, and unconditional acceptance. Any guidance you may offer needs to be done from this view point. As you grow to revere yourself, the world becomes a place of miracles.

A baby comes to earth, sparkling new, filled with God's love, wrapped in an aura of color and sound. It has picked its name and birthday carefully. These are *not accidents*, for the name and birthday provide the knowledge of this soul's past life experiences and growth accomplished, plus the complete plan for this life.

Free Will

So, where does free will enter into all this? Numerology is capable of laying out a blueprint of a person's life. Let's compare it to a Monopoly board. Before our birth, we sit somewhere, maybe in heaven, with our board of advisors. Together we pick our time and place of birth, our sex, parents, sibling order, country, and the name as part of the package. We agree to it, and shazam! A new baby is born! Those things represent our gameboard. From that structure, we are free to pick our "Chance" and "Opportunity" cards, go directly to Jail, pass Go, get $200.00, buy houses, hotels, lose and accumulate wealth, whatever—it's all part of our game. We are free to make our own choices. A big choice is called attitude. I remember my brother would get so angry he'd knock everything off the board—I'd go away crying. To this day, I don't really enjoy playing Monopoly because I have buried somewhere in my subconscious that I'll lose! Looking back on it, I always played defensively. Now, as I grow older, I've learned it's my game, and I'm free to play any position I want. That's a big change in *attitude*.

So the name and birthday set out the game board, and we get to choose how we want to handle each move. Free will is a precious ingredient that needs to be well guarded. Beware of anyone who tries to take it away from you, and also be attentive that you don't attempt to interfere in anyone else's process. Numerology can't accurately predict what choices a person will make because everyone always has the option to change.

Life on Earth is actually a schoolhouse. And in some mysterious way, each decision we make is part of the plan. All choices lead the way into alternative realities and offer opportunities for learning our perfect lessons. Whatever we choose opens the perfect path for learning what we came to learn. There really is no such thing as the "perfect choice" in one sense, and in another, they are all perfect. All choices will have their own set of problems and opportunities built in. Going along with *attitude,* we have another choice which can be called *altitude.* We are free to choose a limited perspective or an unlimited one. I remember years ago a friend whose only child was killed suddenly in a one-car accident. In his grief, the father turned to a stronger faith than he'd ever had before. I could say, "What a meaningless death," or I could see the importance the impact had for the father and appreciate it in a completely different way. In fact, recently I heard he'd become a minister, so now countless people are being helped by that experience. That one death had great meaning when I could see it from a higher perspective.

The numbers, symbolic of everything in life, can be positive or negative. This is probably another way of looking at attitude and altitude. The negative side could be too much or not enough. For instance, the number 1 challenges an individual to live life with courage; too much can make them pig-headed and unbending, not enough and they may be too unsure of themselves to attempt anything new. Usually, the more evolved a soul is, the more positively they live. Another example: 2 on the positive is a peacemaker; on the negative, it can be manipulative or fearful.

My tendency is to look at most things as positive. In the long run, they usually are. Some of us tend towards great impatience with life, unwilling to allow things to unfold in their own way. It reminds me that before Walt Disney's time, animation was achieved by rapidly flicking a deck of cards. We'd see a sexy lady stripping off a tiny bit of her clothes with the movement of each subsequent card. Some of us have a tendency to stop at each card and gasp, forgetting there are more cards still unflipped. Numerology has been a great help in allowing me to see that what looks negative at one time may later turn out to be the best thing that could have happened. So the biggest choice we really have is how loving can we be, and how much fun can we have with the whole process?

ℵ

Importance of the Name

Do we pick our name or does our name pick us? What is more personally ours than our name? When you see a person with your same name, how do you feel? In Bali, parents name their children in sibling order. It's possible to know, from the name, which child is the first-born, second, third, or fourth. Throughout the country, many boys and girls have identical names and there is a great sense of community and family closeness. In Biblical times, each person had an original name unique to them. Throughout time, names have been used as identification. Some were used to describe who we belonged to (John's son), what we did (Tailor), or where we came from (Goldberg—gold mountain). Others have meanings descriptive of our powers (Running Eagle) or energies or qualities it is hoped we'll develop (Rose, Blossom, Charity, Hope). "El" is a name for God and has a powerful significance, such as Lionel. If there is a birth certificate, even if the nurse "made a mistake," whatever is on there is the numbers that have been chosen. No matter how many times a name is changed, the full name at birth remains as the foundation.

First names and first vowels symbolize a source of our power. It's common to see children given nicknames to soften the high energies they are carrying. They usually drop those names as they mature. Yet, it's hard for the friends and loved ones to drop it as this would make it necessary for them to change their view of the person. Whatever name is called represents how we are seen. Changing the name is a very big step as it signifies the readiness for a new life. When God renamed Abram in the Bible, he added an "H" (or 8) and another "A" (or 1) which made him Abraham, and added great power unto him.

The full name at birth represents our foundation and is a source of great strength. While names can be changed countless times, the confidence necessary to make those changes can be attributed to our birth name. We are the sum total of ALL of our experiences, not just those we enjoy remembering. First names, along with first vowels, are potent forces that carry us through to success. Rely on their value and draw upon them as allies. Middle names can be considered as hidden potentials and may perhaps be a well-concealed part of our strength. Total it (or them) and incorporate it more fully. Last names represent family connections and are a bond shared with the entire family. Men who are named after their fathers as Juniors, III's or IV's, have a tremendous bond with those who have gone before them. Jr. adds one extra 1 and one extra 9; everything else is identical. (However, note if Junior is spelled out, and use if that way.) When I read the chart of a Jr., I look at the numbers with the added 1 and 9 and without them, taking both sets of numbers into consideration. I've never known what to do with III's and IV's.

In the alphabet, the first row of letters, A through I, are symbolic of energies of the fullest intensity; J through R are more mature, mellow and understanding. The last row, S through Z, represents the old wise ones who are able to handle more and be philosophical about life.

Importance of the Birthday

So while the name can be changed, and usually is at some point in most lifetimes, the birthday seldom changes. (There are cases of this, but it's usually a "secret" thing, to hide someone's age —making them older or younger—or once in a while, for various reasons, you'll run across someone who really isn't sure when they were born.) If there are two dates in question, the Birthpath of each date and Pinnacles and Challenges can all help as determining factors. Stay clear of giving "advice" or making other people's decisions. There is a big difference in explaining what "the trend" of the situation is—and where things COULD be going, as opposed to speaking in absolutes; i.e., using the words "must" and "have to." In the first place, you don't really know what's the best thing for anyone to be doing—except yourself. In the second, we are all here to make our own choices (refer to the section on Free Will).

Birthdays contain all the cycles we work within and are great sources of helpful information. Some people use them for "divining the future"—I shy away from that, as I could be restricting a person's future or "programming" them with my perspective. We are living in exciting times, where our future is only limited by our imagination. Things are happening in a matter of days that formerly took years. As everything becomes more accelerated, so does our potential for change. People are now able to make dramatic, overnight, life-changing shifts.

So if you're not giving advice, how can this help others?

I've seen real healing take place by a person knowing their life lesson and realizing they are actually learning it. We spend so much of our life wondering if we took the "right" path or made the "right" decision. It's always right somehow. Over the years of working with people, it's been interesting to see when I tell them what they were working on that they can tell me the specifics of it. Use this knowledge to heal yourself, to take away the guilt. I remember a client who called me a week or so after our session together. She said over the intervening weekend she had experienced a whole gamut of emotions. First she felt angry, and frustrated with the people who had turned her into a "victim," then the resentments came forward; finally, she realized it was her life to live as she wanted, and she was ready to take it on, and please herself. At which point, she moved into loving appreciation of everyone in her life, thereby stepping into her own power to choose. Her Birthpath was "1," and as I recall, she had finally come into a "1" Pinnacle, or Challenge. Whatever it takes to get us where we're going—the Pinnacle and Challenge points the way.

ⱬ

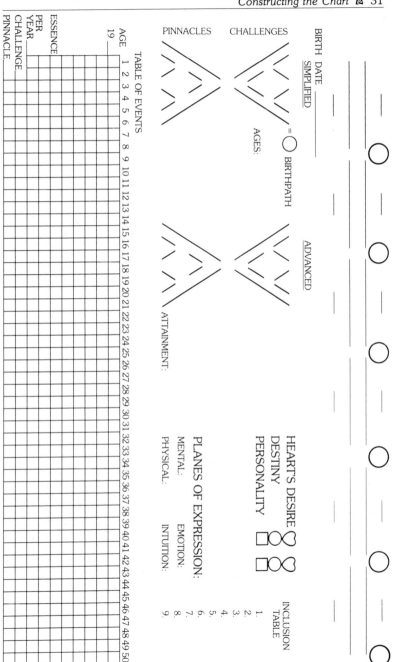

BIRTH DATE
SIMPLIFIED

ADVANCED

= ◯ BIRTHPATH

AGES:

CHALLENGES

PINNACLES

ATTAINMENT:

HEART'S DESIRE
DESTINY
PERSONALITY

INCLUSION
TABLE
1.
2.
3.
4.
5.
6.
7.
8.
9.

PLANES OF EXPRESSION:

MENTAL: EMOTION:

PHYSICAL: INTUITION:

TABLE OF EVENTS

AGE	1	2	3	4	5	6	7	8	9	10	11	12	13	14	15	16	17	18	19	20	21	22	23	24	25	26	27	28	29	30	31	32	33	34	35	36	37	38	39	40	41	42	43	44	45	46	47	48	49	50
19																																																		

ESSENCE

PER
YEAR

CHALLENGE

PINNACLE

BIRTH DATE _____

SIMPLIFIED _____ | _____

CHALLENGES

PINNACLES

AGES: = ◯ BIRTHPATH

ADVANCED

ATTAINMENT: _____

AGE
19 —

TABLE OF EVENTS

1 2 3 4 5 6 7 8 9 10 11 12 13 14 15 16 17 18 19 20 21 22 23 24 25 26 27 28 29 30 31 32 33 34 35 36 37 38 39 40 41 42 43 44 45 46 47 48 49 50

ESSENCE

PER YEAR

CHALLENGE

PINNACLE

PINNACLE _____

CHALLENGE _____

HEART'S DESIRE
DESTINY
PERSONALITY

PLANES OF EXPRESSION:

MENTAL: _____ EMOTION: _____

PHYSICAL: _____ INTUITION: _____

INCLUSION
TABLE

1.
2.
3.
4.
5.
6.
7.
8.
9.

BIRTH DATE

SIMPLIFIED

ADVANCED

= ○ BIRTHPATH

AGES:

CHALLENGES

PINNACLES

ATTAINMENT:

HEART'S DESIRE

DESTINY

PERSONALITY

PLANES OF EXPRESSION:

MENTAL:

EMOTION:

PHYSICAL:

INTUITION:

INCLUSION TABLE

1.
2.
3.
4.
5.
6.
7.
8.
9.

TABLE OF EVENTS

AGE	1	2	3	4	5	6	7	8	9	10	11	12	13	14	15	16	17	18	19	20	21	22	23	24	25	26	27	28	29	30	31	32	33	34	35	36	37	38	39	40	41	42	43	44	45	46	47	48	49	50
19 ___																																																		
ESSENCE																																																		
PER YEAR																																																		
CHALLENGE																																																		
PINNACLE																																																		

BIRTH DATE

SIMPLIFIED

ADVANCED

CHALLENGES

PINNACLES

AGES:

= ◯ BIRTHPATH

ATTAINMENT:

HEART'S DESIRE
DESTINY
PERSONALITY

PLANES OF EXPRESSION:

MENTAL: EMOTION:
PHYSICAL: INTUITION:

INCLUSION
TABLE

1.
2.
3.
4.
5.
6.
7.
8.
9.

TABLE OF EVENTS

AGE
19 —

ESSENCE
PER YEAR
CHALLENGE
PINNACLE
PINNACLE
CHALLENGE

1 2 3 4 5 6 7 8 9 10 11 12 13 14 15 16 17 18 19 20 21 22 23 24 25 26 27 28 29 30 31 32 33 34 35 36 37 38 39 40 41 42 43 44 45 46 47 48 49 50

BIRTH DATE _____

SIMPLIFIED

ADVANCED

= ◯ BIRTHPATH

AGES:

CHALLENGES

PINNACLES

ATTAINMENT:

HEART'S DESIRE

DESTINY

PERSONALITY

INCLUSION TABLE

1.
2.
3.
4.
5.
6.
7.
8.
9.

PLANES OF EXPRESSION:

MENTAL: EMOTION:

PHYSICAL: INTUITION:

TABLE OF EVENTS

AGE	1	2	3	4	5	6	7	8	9	10	11	12	13	14	15	16	17	18	19	20	21	22	23	24	25	26	27	28	29	30	31	32	33	34	35	36	37	38	39	40	41	42	43	44	45	46	47	48	49	50
19																																																		

ESSENCE

PER YEAR

CHALLENGE

PINNACLE

A Complete Introduction to the Numbers

Approach these symbols as if they were completely new to you, so you can see them with new eyes. These are symbols of the sacred, divine energies that are being manifested on the planet. Treat them with great respect and understanding as befitting their importance. They are grouped as "even" numbers and "odd" numbers, because this is how they are the most complementary. Each number generally has a problem with the one next to it as the numbers grate against each other. In time edges get sanded down until they all interlock, fitting together and complementing each other.

ℵ

The

Odd

Numbers

1   3   5   7   9

Odd numbers represent the intangibles: creativity, flair, inspiration, love of adventure. They like to expand the form of things. They don't like to fit in and sometimes stop right in the middle and and change direction.

Even numbers want to maintain the form, odd numbers want to expand it. In the past, this meant lots of struggles and headaches. In the future, this will mean lots of expansion and growth. There is a concept that stress is to be expected and necessary for growth. While that may be, getting into the flow with it is the dance of life, or the Tao. They can dance in and out of each other, or fight to hang on to their way being the "only way."

1

Key Words

1's key word is *courage*; its symbol, a flame; it radiates the colors of a flame and sings the musical note of C. Gemstones and minerals that vibrate to 1 are aquamarine, moss agate, turquoise, and copper. Its flower is lilac. The 1 is a strong, independent symbol representing a true channel for the Word of God. 1 stands with its two feet firmly on the ground, its head in the clouds, listening only to the voice of the inner teacher.

Attributes

Strong will power, determination, originality, independence, leadership abilities, poineering spirit, unique individuality.

Usual Tendencies of Behavior

1s tend to be loners, someone ahead of their time, always having new ideas for starting things; wanting things to go their way. Or, they are interested in new fields where they feel the challenge of beginning new ventures. They are the innovators, the idea-people in life. Some very definitely may be able to relate to the title of leader, and some may not. There are those who just see a need and fill it, or have a strong desire to give something a try, while other people sit and watch, wondering what they're doing now, and why (and then may later "give it a try" themselves). Frequently the 1 doesn't really set out to be a leader, any more than the pioneers set out to open all areas of our country for us to come two hundred years later and build communities—1's just see a new way and are courageous enough to try it. 1's can look at others and wonder why they are such sheep.

In the Past

1 had a strong tendency to be pigheaded, not only wanting things to go its way, but expecting others to approve and under-

stand its ideas. It frequently would not listen to others' viewpoints or had a chip on its shoulder, maybe feeling sorry for itself that it was so different and so individual, sometimes provoking arguments from the need to "prove" things to others. 1's were not great at "sharing."

In the Future

1 will be more centered inside itself, knowing approval of self is more important than others' approval. It will be more loving and accepting of the great opportunity it has to live its life with no role models, tuned only inside itself to the voice of God. It will know the importance of completely accepting and believing in itself—understanding its service is to know itself, its wants, needs and desires, and how to fill them, then have the satisfaction of seeing others benefit from this clear sense of direction. My grandmother used to say grandpa only thought of "Number One." That's true with a 1. Yet, the future 1 will be more gentle with others. They will be centered, heart to heart with God.

Conflicts with Other Numbers

1's area of conflict with other numbers is simply that the 1 usually wants to be the leader or do things in its own fashion. This is pretty much okay with all the other odd numbers (except another 1); however, it's not so okay with most of the even numbers. Mostly it's fine with the 2, who is the team person and needs a leader, yet sometimes there may be seething resentments about being told what to do all the time. The 4 likes things very structured and might object to 1 constantly having more new ideas than the 4 can fit into all its little boxes and files; the 6 might see it as irresponsible, always to be off to something new before the old job is completed; the 8 likes to direct and control, so there could easily be a power struggle between 1 and 8—8 needing to prove its way is right, and 1 with an original new plan it wants to see put into action. Also, both numbers stand up strongly and are very outspoken about their opinions of how things need to operate.

Lessons to be Learned

• To listen to its own inner guidance and believe in itself enough to act on it.

- To realize others' opinions are only other opinions.
- To stand centered on its own two feet and live valiantly.
- To believe in itself and realize that no matter how well-loved it is, no other number can really understand what it is trying to accomplish. The only source of reliable guidance for a trailblazer comes from inside.
- To be aware that other people are different—and that's fine.

People Skills You Might Want to Develop

The ability to be a little more patient with those around, to pause every now and then so others can come a little closer. Remember, 1 is the leader who leads through actions, not just words, learning to listen and give freely of its ideas without the sense that things can only be done as originally planned. 1 represents the idea-person; others need those ideas before they can carry out their part, which is the next step. This is why 1's may not be acknowledged or even remembered for their contributions, yet all can appreciate and benefit from them. Being a 1 can often be a thankless job; maybe as it remembers to thank others more often (including and especially God) it may be thanked more frequently in return. 1's are the Johnny Appleseeds of life, and need to be aware that is a blessing.

Talents

You are a starter, an idea person, an innovator; if you start out in a job where you are part of a team, you will somehow usually work it until you are the boss (whether others notice or not). You do best as your own person. Your skills are in breaking ground for others who come behind. Read all books, take any classes, work with affirmations, do whatever you can to empower and encourage yourself to stand independently and do it "your way." In this, you will set the example, creating a world of unique individuals who are living their lives freely.

If You Have a 1 Birthpath

All of the above is the life lesson. Your life experiences will be structured to get you to know you are worthy and capable. Make a flash card that says "Courage" and keep it with you always. Quiz yourself from time to time on what that means to you in this instant or how it would look if you were living it now. Love and appreciate yourself for all the strides you have made in this area, and continually support yourself in this manner. Your life lesson is to believe in yourself, validate yourself, and stand by yourself—always. Any time you are looking to someone else to do this for you, you are giving them power over you and diluting your effectiveness. Your "mistakes" turn into new avenues of expression. No one knows better than you what's best for you.

If You Have a 1 Destiny

If your Fairy Godmother had tapped you on the forehead with her wand and said, "Be valiant in your dedication to honesty and integrity as you live courageously," your feet would have been pointed along the correct path. You have been picked to be a leader in life, and agreed to take on the role. This may not look like you think, as there is no role model. The only mistake is to look outside yourself to get an idea of the way in which others do things. What you see is their way. Time and again, you will be reminded that your way is different. Stride into the adventure of this! Johnny Appleseed spent his time sowing seeds abundantly, not having a sense of how many would come up—or where. There is great freedom in this concept.

Heart's Desire

To have a 1 heart desire is like the lion in the *Wizard of Oz* going to the Wizard for more courage. With a 1, the only way to have more courage is to stride into it and "act as if you do." Your heart lies in the path of purity and integrity and living true to the teachings of your inner guidance. Your heart is happiest starting new projects and blazing new trails, not when you are doing the time-tested, well-proven. Make that okay, and tune into the God within, as that's the only One upon whom you can rely. Staying out of your ego and staying tuned to God may call upon you to demonstrate valor and fearlessness in the face of opposition. See them as opportunities to strengthen. If you live your life with integrity, you will be doing it "your way" and that will encourage others to do the same.

Pinnacle

The 1 pinnacle is asking you to demonstrate leadership abilities, being out front and courageous with your opinions and ideas. It's a time for thinking new and original thoughts, acknowledging your Divine guidance, and having the strength to act on it. This is a powerful time. Stand in your strength, and compare yourself to no one. Center inside. Be assertive. Most of all, accept yourself exactly as you are RIGHT NOW. When you criticize yourself, you are criticizing God. That means complete acceptance, from your hair down to your toenails—no complaints. Acceptance is one of the first laws of this planet. As you can offer it to yourself and others, everyone will thrive.

Challenge

The challenge of a 1 is to stand independently and live courageously. It is a time to listen only inside so that you are living fully. This can look eccentric, and often be difficult for friends and loved ones to understand. They say: "You always have to do it your way." Yes, your challenge is to learn what IS your way and to demonstrate to yourself that it works. "I should have listened to myself." It's true; anytime you are looking outside yourself for approval, you are giving your power to someone else. This is a special time to be finding YOU, believing, validating, and approving of yourself—not looking to others to do that for you. The only person who can live your life is you. Watch as your "mistakes" lead into creating innovative methods and approaches to things never attempted before you came along. You may see others benefit from your ideas as if you are shining a light into the darkness, illuminating many areas. Perhaps you'll notice others using your ideas as their own. That's fine; you are the idea person. Remember, they couldn't have done what they've done without your contribution to open the way. Be aware that when you look to others for approval, they're not capable of giving it to you. Your job is to stay balanced and centered inside yourself; realize 1 is the number that represents God and that your real challenge is to move into the part of you that is God, that creates endlessly anew. Your challenge is to know yourself, what you want from life, and how to achieve it.

Home play. Look into your eyes in the mirror, and repeat for seven days: "I love you, [your name]. I support you, [your name]. I believe in you, [your name]. The God within me is always working for the highest good."

Attainment

1 is to achieve an abundance of inner strength and personal power. It is to attain "oneness" with God and live with great integrity and courage. This may indicate unexpected leadership abilities in areas you pioneer. Allow others to use your ideas freely for their purposes. Guard against being domineering or dominating.

Law of Opposites

Pythagoras' first law of fundamental opposites is Limited and Unlimited. The 1 represents the Sun and is considered masculine, the right hemisphere, the intellect.

Words That Total 1

Integrity, spirit, sunshine, sincere. In the alphabet, $A = 1$, $J = 10$, $S = 19$; all reduce to 1.

3

Key Words

The key words for 3 are *joy* and *creativity*; it radiates the colors of orchid, and royal blue. 3 sings the note of D; its symbol is the triangle $\triangle$. Gems and minerals are lavish, as would be appropriate for a number representing creativity: amber, luvulite, lapis lazuli, amethyst, quartz, and cadmium. The rose is the flower for 3.

Attributes

3's attributes are, first and foremost, its joy. I've always loved the fact there is a number that represents joy. And from that joy comes boundless creativity. This is a playful number; lucky, easy-going, it has a great sense of humor, and this fact eases all its dealings in life. It is childlike and innocent with a sunny disposition, has a way with words, and a great imagination.

Usual Tendencies of Behavior

Usual tendencies are to enjoy life and living and not take things too seriously. 3 can be messy and fill spaces with creative clutter, jumping from one project to another with a strong urge to not complete anything unless it's really interested. It tends to giggle at the most inopportune moments (which it sometimes learns to suppress as it grows older). 3 can be artistic, talkative, and love to be in the middle of a group of people having fun.

In the Past

In the past, 3 frequently got squashed by other numbers for being frivolous and silly, being told to "grow up," "act your age," "stop day-dreaming," and "take life seriously." This diminished its sense of joy considerably, as you can imagine. It was also labeled "the cock-eyed optimist" and "Pollyanna," labels which were all appropriate except they usually sounded so negative. As 3 was learning to be a communicator, it often had trouble expressing its true feelings, and frequently used so many words others got lost in what it was trying to express.

In the Future

In the future, 3 will understand its strength comes from its ability to imagine a positive future and use its imagination liberally to create it. It will be able to stay in the present and find the perfect word to communicate straight from its heart. Its joy will lift and inspire others to be more creative, with great emphasis on trying something simply for fun and approaching it playfully, as a child does before it starts wanting to look grown-up and serious. "And a little child shall lead them…" 3 will see its ability to lighten up and laugh as being a service to everyone, and comprehend that these are healing powers.

Conflicts With Other Numbers

3's greatest conflicts come from numbers who judge them as flighty. 1 tries to boss the 3, and is allowed to until 3 goes on to something more fun. 2's and 4's feel quite insecure when they can't put 3's pieces together or organize them; 5's and 3's are similar to each other and get along well unless they are judging each other on the thing most other numbers judge them on: staying with something only as long as their interest holds out. 6 is a grown-up 3, and so can see the 3 as irresponsible; 7 can conflict drastically as it is a serious number and 3 wants to have fun; 8 judges 3 as wasting time in life, not accomplishing anything, not "going anywhere." 9 could feel 3 "should" do something more significant with itself than just express its joy, not realizing what an important service that is to all.

Lessons to be Learned
• To stay in the moment and be joyful.
• When expressing itself, to come as close as possible to conveying the message of its heart.
• To do those things that lift it, so that through its joy it can lift and inspire others. It is learning that laughter and humor are special graces which heal all sorts of tensions and stress. The 3 is filled with an endless source of creativity which needs to be brought into the world. Everyone stands to benefit if it will continually cultivate new solutions to old problems and approach all things with a smile.

People Skills You Might Want to Develop
As 3 communicates on many levels, including the words, do those things that will assist you to be comfortable as a public speaker and/or writer. Approach this joyfully, not as some big serious task that needs to be conquered. Do whatever is necessary to relieve yourself of the past so that you can stay in the moment and be happy with yourself and your life. Develop the skill of making everything you do be fun; learn to smile from your heart.

Talents
Your talents lie in any field of creativity, music, art, healing arts, communication. Wherever you enjoy being and a sunny disposition is needed, you will have a contribution to make.

If You Have a 3 Birthpath

Your life lesson is to fully and freely utilize your imagination and make everything you do an expression of joy. Attempt to see the humor in each situation, no matter how hard you need to look. The big cosmic joke is that we all take things so seriously. Did you ever realize the similarity between cosmic and comic? Develop your imagination by practicing visualizing on the inner screens of your mind, and use that as a tool to create your world as you want it. Don't buy into others' ideas of how it "has to be." That's their reality; it's only yours if you agree to accept it. Create a reality for yourself of how it *could be* at its most wonderful. Let that be an image that grows with each day, unhampered by all the restrictions others place on themselves—that is not your path in life. Challenge yourself to lift out of any negativity. Your life lesson is to let your child come out and play. Constantly push yourself for greater creativity—even if you know how to do something, invent a new way.

If You Have a 3 Destiny

If your Fairy Godmother had tapped you on the forehead and said, "Dear child, play with life as a joyous gift and constantly share the love in your heart through artistic expressions," your feet would have been pointed on the correct path. You are here to demonstrate that you are a child of God, playing with life and having great fun doing it. Share that fun with others and assist them to see that life may have been hard and serious in the times gone by, yet the future holds wonders of unlimited joy and free expression of creativity. As you create, know that your creations are completely yours. Only you can have your babies or hatch your eggs. For each person in the world there is an expression only they can make. No one can write your poem, tell your story, think the same thought, observe a color, or even handle a situation in exactly the same manner. You are sprouting the seeds that Johnny Appleseed was sowing; don't curtail that in any way. When you speak, center in your heart and bring out your true feelings in lightness and joy... "out of the mouths of babes come words or wisdom." Most of all, lighten up and enjoy your life. Your service is to your inner child, to bring out that sense of delight and wonderment.

Heart's Desire

Your heart's desire is joy. A little child lives inside your heart and needs to be able to come out and play regularly. Stiffled away, the child pouts and finds ways to take revenge on you for allowing that to happen. The results of this could be disastrous. To avoid any such dire consequences, make play, fun and good times a regular part of your life. Approach life playfully, lighten up and giggle whenever necessary, and please, don't ever allow yourself to think you are a "grown up;" that's not much fun at all. Approach life as a creative exercise and see how much originality and creativity you can put into everything you do. Inspire yourself to be positive, and encourage those around you to play with you — let them be like you rather than you like them!

Pinnacle

The 3 pinnacle is a *charmed* time of your life where you have talents and abilities for things you never suspected — push through your first little steps and bumble into learning anything you ever thought would be fun to try. Go back into your childhood and make a list of twenty-five things you enjoyed doing and see how many are being incorporated into your life today. Add some, and open new channels for your creativity to emerge. Approach it child-like, without any big sense of how good you are or where it will go. The goal is to open your own creativity and allow it to shine out to the world. Your personal expression is solely yours. Don't compare what you do with anything you've seen, heard, or otherwise noticed of others. Their's is not yours. Look for new opportunities to be creative and approach everything with a sense of joy and humor. Allow your inner child to play; your creative imagination is your source of strength.

Challenge

The challenge of the three is joy! So allow the child in you to show. This challenge is to lighten up and laugh at life, and bring that humor with you into every situation. A smile achieves more inner peace and balance than countless words. You are being challenged to know that you are truly a child of God, and be able to express that in joyful creativity. Be positive and use your words carefully to inspire and lift yourself and others to greater heights. "Gravity" only needs to hold us down physically. This is a time of expansion, so your life dance can be a freer expression rather than a dirge or processional. This is a very special challenge; open all your levels of creativity and express through the arts, writing, singing, dancing, healing arts, some special expression that only you can make. No matter if it is a flower arrangement, a special meal, a drawing; no one will ever do it exactly as you do.

Home play: Look in the mirror and watch what happens as you smile. Smile at a stranger and see his or her face light up. Smile in the middle of a business argument, laugh at yourself for taking it so seriously; watch the energy shift. Amazingly, interesting studies have been done on the power of laughter as a tool for healing. See Norman Cousins' *Anatomy of an Illness.*

Attainment

3 is to achieve a joyful outlook on life and live it easily with an abundance of spontaneity, creativity, and originality. It is to express positive thoughts that inspire and lift others. This may indicate opportunities to speak or write. Guard against scattering your words and thoughts. Polish them until they shine with the exact meaning you intend.

Law of Opposites

Pythagoras' fundamental law of opposites is the One and the Many.

Words That Total 3

Freedom, build, angel, glow. In the alphabet, C = 3, L = 12, U = 21, all reduce to 3.

5

Key Word

The key word for 5 is *expansion*. It radiates the color of pink and sings the musical note of E. Its symbol is a five-pointed star.

Gemstones and minerals are carnelian, alexandrite, lapidilite, tiger's eye, chrysocolla, and clay. The flowers are carnations and sweet peas.

Attributes

5 is called the *curiosity of mankind* and wants to experience everything life has to offer. It is a very sensual number wanting to experience through its senses; that means smelling, touching, hearing, seeing, and tasting all of life, plus wanting to explore through all of the extra senses as well. 5 has a hard time making choices because it wants a little of everything. It is quick to learn, expansive, changeable, eccentric, eclectic, enthusiastic, dynamic, versatile, and difficult to define because the only thing consistent about 5 is its inconsistency. It is a great talker and gifted salesperson.

Usual Tendencies of Behavior

The usual tendency of the 5 is to be unusual. 5 is the number of expansion and unlimitedness and does those things in every direction — at all times. Just like the fingers of the hand, 5's attention and interest go in all directions, and as it is the middle number (between 1 to 9), it is in the middle of all things. With these characteristics, more can be written about a 5 than any other number. 5 is unpredictable and changeable except on one basic issue: 5 wants to be free to be itself without any restrictions or limitations. It says, "Don't fence me in," has a difficult time committing to anything, and frequently doesn't trust itself. Even the 5 sometimes has trouble handling being so different from any other number. 5 wants to make its own choices. 5's are attractive to both sexes, and usually stay that way regardless of age. They are open to life and willing to try almost anything. And yet, they can have great fears that prevent them from doing anything. 5 is the adventurer in life and is not very concerned with accumulating possessions or wealth. It can be very generous, restless, and impatient.

In the Past

Although the 5 has appeared fearless, it frequently had incredible fears that have prevented it from having more of the experiences it wanted. Many times 5 tried to look more accountable and dependable, to conform itself to the ways of others. My private joke to myself is that our last instruction as we were leaving heaven was, "Watch them and just do what everyone else does!" So, being unpredictable and always wanting to do the off-beat, Bohemian thing; having interests no one shared; not wanting what everyone else was placing great value on; it was easy for the 5 to get confused.

In the Future

5 really has a very important role in life as it is "the expander." It pushes the buttons of all the other numbers when it comes to freedom. Wanting freedom at any cost, is paid for by letting go enough to be different. This number is taking us into the future as it carries change, new ideas, and progress with it everywhere. Some numbers welcome this. Some are afraid. Regardless, the 5 continues to live its life unconventionally and communicate about it. (Actually, this book is being written from the viewpoint of 5). A secret to letting go is to turn life into a series of experiences without judging any of their rightness or wrongness, just living them all. 5 is helping to create a world with no fear by taking the risks and breaking the conventions and letting others see that it's all okay.

Conflicts With Other Numbers

It has intrigued me how judgmental other numbers can be of the 5. Of course it's the even numbers that are the most critical. Even in Numerology books, 5's are described as flaky, foolish, undependable, unstable, and have been told this in one form or another throughout their life. Being told they never finish what they start and can't be counted on is pretty harsh. 5 does the things other numbers wish they could, and touches everyone's life with change. 5 can't be a conformist, even when it tries, so it turns out that 5 is the number that keeps loosening its hold on life, and setting the example, both through words and actions, of a life of expansion into a world with no fears.

Lessons to be Learned
• To live life, letting go of all fear, apprehension, and concern with the past or the future.
• To do things in moderation (a word the 5 barely knows).

- To profit from others' experiences every now and then — without having to try everything.
- To hold life loosely.
- To be flexible and to discern between where to hold on and what to drop. Let the words "choose" and "prefer" replace the words "should" and "ought to" in your inner dialogues.

People Skills You Might Want to Develop

5's impatience can be difficult for everyone involved. Try slowing down and being a triffle more deliberate. The more patience you can bring into a situation, the more often you may see available choices otherwise missed. Practice focusing your full attention in the moment and see how much more will be accomplished. Restlessness and boredom are not always undesirable, learn to hang in there, allowing life to unfold, rather than doing something "dumb" just for novelty.

If You Have a 5 Birthpath

5's life lesson is to expand into this life, to smell it, touch it, hear, see, taste and live it fully, to learn that freedom is running to things as well as running away from them. It is to realize that life is a continual series of choices, and even wrong ones can be valuable. Since 5 learns about life from a completely experiential viewpoint, it learns little by taking another's advice. The 5 needs to make its own mistakes so that it can profit from them. Life is a series of possible realities, with each small choice a decision of which path to explore. 5 wants to explore all pathways. Its life is filled with sudden changes and unexpected opportunities, demanding great flexibility. 5 is not about holding onto the past and reliving it, it is about exploration and liberation. Freedom comes as the 5 learns it is not any other number — and couldn't be, even if it tried. Value each sensation for the learning it offers, and stay focused in the present moment to obtain the full benefits.

If You Have a 5 Destiny

If your Fairy Godmother had touched your forehead at birth with her magic wand and said, "You are a free spirit, here to live the fullness of life," your feet would be striding along the correct path. This path is not really about taking advice from others, or doing things their way. It is about exploring the highways and byways of life and having all the adventures. Without 5's, no one would have pushed the limits of the tired and well-known blueprints for living. No automobiles, no space exploration, no one willing to take a risk anywhere. You have a very important job, and that is to communicate change wherever you go. You are expanding others' horizons as well as allowing them the opportunity to view life without restrictions and limitations. This can place fear in lots of hearts. People won't always welcome you with open arms. You may reflect things that make them uncomfortable. Throughout all of time, there have always been troubadours, wandering minstrels, and storytellers singing their songs, telling stories of battles, other lands, customs and traditions. This encourages the wanderlust in some and expands others with ideas of far-away lands and new ways. This is you in modern garb, and your job is more important now than ever. We are on the way to becoming a unified world, filled with a tremendous variety of colors, sizes, shapes, and languages. Lots of mind-sets and stereotypical views need to change to allow this to happen. You are perfect for the job. Just be positive, and know it's all going to turn out fine.

Heart's Desire

Your heart's desire is to be free from the old tapes and unconscious programming you've accumulated of *others'* value systems and ideas of what is important in life. Your goal is to be free to choose to live in the moment. While you may have a strong desire to travel everywhere and experience everything, you may also have a tug on your heart to have the adventure of a true commitment in staying put. It all becomes a matter of choice. No path is superior to another, as long as the choice is in your able hands and you realize that "mistakes" are nothing more than *other* experiences.

Pinnacle

The 5 pinnacle: Open all the channels to free expression and clear communication. This is a time for great exploration and adaptation to the unexpected. A small interest or hobby could blossom into a whole new career or way of life. Demonstrate your "jack of all trades-ness" and don't try to be predictable. If you listen closely, you may hear yourself expressing new opinions that surprise you. Read any new thing that catches your eye, take any classes that interest you. Think about travel on any plane of existence, and encourage yourself to go for the adventures that life has to offer. Be ready to seize any new opportunity that *feels right* without analyzing why or where it will lead. Curiosity may have killed the cat, but the cat also had nine lives—choose any metaphor you like and remember, this time of your life is about endless choices and unlimited freedom. Analyze your old tapes and unconscious programming by listening to yourself and your opinions. If you think you can't do something, ask yourself why not? If it's a good reason—fine. If it's no longer valid, you might want scrap it. Make a point of learning something trivial or small each day!

Challenge

The challenge of 5 is for great freedom and expansion in your life; open to new ideas, risks, and adventures on every level. See all you encounter as "experiences," without qualifying them as "good" or "bad," simply that they are "another experience." Your challenge is one of flexibility. Pause before you do something from habit and look for a new approach; realize there are not just two ways to do things, but always *countless* methods. Try being the exception to the rule. Monitor your thoughts and find some new ones to think. Try something sheerly for the adventure of it.

Home play: Try coloring in a colorbook going OUTSIDE the lines. Eat a new food, wear some new color, speak to a stranger. Deliberately do something that you said you would never do. Love yourself through your fears. Break an old habit.

Attainment

5 is to become more open, attractive, and flexible as you grow older. It is to have greater curiosity about the world, enhanced by the desire to travel and learn. This may indicate sudden changes with opportunity continuing to knock forever. Guard against the notion that you are "too old to...."

Law of Opposites

Pythagoras' fundamental law of opposites: Male and Female. Pythagoras held 5 in high esteem and considered the letter Y special as it represented choice.

Words that Total 5

Language, fairy, power, fantasy. In the alphabet, E = 5, N = 14, W = 23; all reduce to 5.

7

The numbers 1 through 6 represent the cares and concerns of the everyday world, sometimes called the mundane. 7 is a magical, mystical number, and has very special properties. In the Judeo-Christian version of creation, God made the world in six days and on the seventh He rested. He didn't really rest. He surveyed all that He had created and saw that it was good. So he studied, analyzed, criticized, declared it finished, and started planning to go back to work on Monday. 7 stands as the space for quiet and peace. It can bridge the higher world with the lower one, bridge the inner world with the outer one, or anything that needs bridging. Standing with each foot in a different place, 7's not really sure where it belongs. Frequently, 7's find themselves in uncommon positions, perhaps as the child of a "mixed marriage" or someone holding opinions and viewpoints that bear no resemblance to those of their peers. Sometimes they try to hide behind silence, thinking that may bridge the gap. It's difficult to camouflage a bridge. 7 symbolizes great dedication, inner strength, wisdom, and tenacity of purpose as these are the tools required for a job that requires much faith.

With the 7, we enter the higher realms of existence; it serves as our bridge.

Key Words

Key words for 7 are *wisdom* and *faith*. It radiates the colors of purple, pearl and brick, and sings the musical note F#. Gemstones and minerals: carbuncle, rose quartz, and agate. It is symbolized by a square and triangle combined ⌂ and the flowers are poppies, geraniums, hyacinths, and sunflowers.

Attributes

7 is the symbol for great mystery, magic, and ceremony. As it opens the door to higher knowledge and understanding, it is extremely dedicated and takes its job seriously. It can appear withdrawn, aloof, introspective, and intense. While it is great at concealing things, keeping secrets, analyzing everything, collecting data and giving the impression of perfection, it also can be brilliant and have incredible intelligence.

Usual Tendencies of Behavior

The 7 is doing a research paper with life as its project. It analyzes everything, seeking great understanding. However, it is also looking for perfection and commonly sees what's wrong rather than what's right. 7 has a great tendency to criticize everything and do nothing to change any of it. It can look superior and complete inside itself, as if it needs nothing from anyone. It is the skeptic, and can be counted on to have great doubts about most things. Even as a child, this number is frequently misunderstood and is a "strange child," keeping secrets and wondering why it's so different. The 7 is usually found off by itself somewhere in nature, or in a corner watching and observing. Even when very lonely, it frequently has a difficult time asking for companionship or accepting things from others.

In the Past

7 was very hidden with its thoughts and feelings, tending to look down on others as being frivolous. It commonly grew up in an atmosphere of aloneness—feeling rejected on one hand, and keeping others out on the other. Probably early in life it noticed its concerns and interests were very different. It usually viewed the world through a magnifying glass, saying "Hmmmmm" a lot, and looking for all the flaws, errors, and imperfections. This was difficult for anyone to live with—especially the 7 itself. The 7, serving as a bridge, stands with one foot in one place and the other in

another, spanning things. This translates to it not being quite of one nor the other and feeling very separate from both. It often looked at the way in which others lived and felt excluded and different, not quite understanding the importance of its own role in life.

In the Future

7 has spent lifetimes questing and accumulating the knowledge and wisdom it now has, preparing for the time this would be needed. The bridge is one of our most important symbols, assisting us to extend into worlds that haven't been joined before. Bridging requires the great strength of purpose and dedication the 7 has developed; it has stood as a lone sentinel, a lighthouse, a beacon —sometimes mistrusting itself and God. Having survived the "dark days of its soul," the 7 of the future will live a life of quiet strength in devotion and absolute trust in God. It will shine its light proudly and share its secret knowledge with all of mankind, speaking truth as it sees it, letting go of its separateness and feeling the praise and admiration of all for a job well done.

Conflicts With Other Numbers

Conflict is not quite the correct term to use with regard to the 7, as 7 is not frequently involved in conflict. It's too much of a loner for that. It avoids conflicts, puts up its walls, and retreats. Because of its unique characteristics, 7 is not well understood by any of the other numbers, although, if it takes the time, it can understand them sometimes better than it does itself. The 7, being so analytical, can understand anything it puts its mind to, and so assumes other numbers have this same ability. The 7 is the hurt person who says, "If you loved me, you'd know," or "I don't need them anyway." 7 gets hurt and feels rejected easily, yet seldom shows it, and this characteristic leads to it feeling sorry for itself and being misunderstood. Other numbers seem to give 7 lots of space and go about their business; only another 7 would really have problems with this. When a 7 feels rejected, it turns around and rejects back—stony silences, or two stone walls battling.

Lessons to be Learned

• When 7 feels alone, left out or rejected, it frequently is causing it, looking for it, or expecting it.

- To want to look perfect at all times may be denying you greater achievement and challenge, which leads to your feeling stifled and bored.
- 7 can analyze things to pieces; try telling yourself that it's all grander than anything you can comprehend, anyway.
- You don't have to be perfect all the time.

People Skills You Might Want to Develop

People skills you might want to develop are around learning to be part of a group or how to vocalize some of your deep needs and desires for companionship. Bear in mind others don't understand you unless you can explain yourself. One of the more difficult things for a 7 to do is open up and share its innermost secrets; yet as it does, it will learn more about that most precious puzzle of all—itself. Inside it, truly lies the microcosm of the universe.

Talents

7's talents lie in any field of scientific research or speculation. They are great with computers or any of the technology of today. Anywhere someone is needed to dig for hidden answers or analyze data, the 7 is the one for the job. They are gifted detectives, students of life, archaeologists, anthropologists, astronomers, deep sea divers, geologists, numerologists, philosophers, metaphysicians, or religionists.

If You Have a 7 Birthpath

In a birthpath, your life lesson is to find faith and trust. All of your life experiences are geared toward this. Your path is that of a loner, as the mysteries you want to solve are solitary pursuits. These days, the 7's are coming out of their caves and hiding places so that you might easily find someone to walk the path next to yours and keep you company. In truth, only deep faith can fill the emptiness you have within.

If You Have a 7 Destiny

If your Fairy Godmother had touched your forehead with her magic wand and said, "Dedicate your life to the pursuit of truth and radiate its brilliance, fearlessly," your feet would have been pointed along the correct path. You are here as a lighthouse for the world, and when you are centered in your heart, you radiate with great brilliance. When you are centered in your intellect, trying to analyze it, rationalize and debate it, it turns into so many words. The world really doesn't need more words right now. It needs dedication to the truth, which is: That God Is. The 7 operates through the Law of Attraction. You are always drawing unto yourself your perfect experiences for growth. See them as perfect and acknowledge frequently you don't recognize perfection until you see it from hindsight. You are here demonstrating faith and trust.

Bring more ceremony into your life, unless it makes you uneasy. Celebrate the conclusion of each day, the rising of the moon, invent your own causes for celebration. You have been a seeker on the path of truth for lifetimes. Dig back into your unconscious and bring forward the wisdom that is stored, waiting there. Although others may be saying similar things, only *you* can utter the words that come from *your* perceptions and experiences. You need a time to be alone by yourself, every day. Everyone benefits if you take it.

Heart's Desire

Your heart's desire is for quiet and to know all the mysteries of the universe. As a child you were the one who loved jigsaw puzzles, codes, solving mysteries, and finding "what's wrong with this picture." Sometimes you are still doing that, with your eye going to the one out-of-place thing and criticizing it. You probably notice every crooked picture, and clutter can be very difficult for you. However, this translates into a strong streak of perfectionism which can be very hard for you and others to live with. There is an emptiness in your heart that can only be filled by faith. The questions your heart asks, "Is there anything to believe in?" "Is there a God?" "Can I trust?" can only be answered by you, with time. Devote yourself to finding those answers, as they are the key to the peace you so desire.

The search for greater wisdom is an endless search; share what you learn as you go. While other numbers do other things, you have the heart of a seeker.

Pinnacle

The 7 pinnacle is a quiet time to turn to the inner planes of knowledge for faith. 7 is seeking the perfection and often can be very critical, seeing only the imperfection. We all can see what's wrong; this is a special time for you to perceive what is right, and with faith and great wisdom understand the plan is always perfect. 7 desires to analyze and understand all things. On some levels that's fine; on others, a little unrealistic as the big plan is so much greater than anything that we can comprehend. Compare it to studing only an inch of a road map and becoming an expert on the whole freeway system. 7 can have a lot of pride, feeling like it needs to appear perfect at all times. This is a time of great exploration into any hidden area of life and detachment from the concerns of the outside worlds. This might look like a desire to enter a convent or study for the priesthood in young people. It can also be a time of great brillance and excellence as a seeker, making huge strides in the pursuit of undiscovered knowledge. It can also feel like going through the dark days of your soul before finally coming out into the Light. Have the faith to drop some of your "perfection" facade and allow the real you to emerge from behind the screen. Fears and doubts are part of the human condition at this time. If you can show yours, others can reveal theirs. We are all truly one, and there's nothing to fear. Take a little time for yourself each day.

Challenge

The challenge of the 7 is of faith and trust, in yourself, in others, and in God. It is a time to actively find real meaning and understanding of life's purpose and plan. This is an important challenge requesting you to make a firmer connection with Spirit. As you find those things that give you peace in your innermost being, you become a bridge with the higher world. It is a time to start meditating, perhaps delving into spiritual, esoteric, and metaphysical literature. The challenge is to turn within for answers, knowing they'll be there. You are studying life at this time, and will notice you have a greater interest in its mysteries. Dig more relentlessly for answers, and accept only your own. The 7 can be an aloof, reserved number, naturally prone to keeping secrets which may result in your feeling very alone, even in company. This aloneness is part of the challenge, as the peace of mind and faith, once found, will be forever. You are the observer of life now, watching and learning from it all. Try moving through your reluctance and sharing your knowledge with others. If you feel shut out, realize it is going both ways.

Home play: Picture yourself living in a world where you are demonstrating the characteristics of trust and faith. What would that look like to you? Try acting that out and feeling what it feels like. Then work on the assumption "what if..." and create a reality where you are safe and secure in the love of God.

Attainment
7 is to achieve a sense of peace and tranquility that emanates from you. It is to know you are spending the remainder of your life developing more faith, the foundation of life on earth. This may indicate a cabin in the woods waiting for you or a special retreat of your own. Guard against feeling sorry for yourself. If you are alone too much, take the initiative to bring others into your sanctuary.

Law of Opposites
Pythagoras' fundamental law of opposites: Crooked and Straight.

Words That Total 7
Excellence, wonder, science, create. In the alphabet, G = 7, P = 16, Y = 25; all reduce to 7.

9

9, the highest of the odd numbers and the symbol for completions. 9 is the 6 grown older, wiser, and much more tolerant of others.

Key Words
Forgiveness and *unconditional love.* 9 radiates the colors of red, brown, lavender, and periwinkle blue. It sings the musical note

of G#. Gems and minerals are berylligure, malachite, nickel, spar, and bone. The symbol is △△, three triangles; flowers are holly and magnolia.

Attributes

9 represents service, beauty, and love on the highest levels. It is the greatest appreciator of the artistry of life, and works to raise mass consciousness to a higher degree through its philanthropic deeds. Having deep concern for all mankind, it is very universal in its outlook and assists through its compassion and understanding.

Usual Tendencies

The 9 tends to live its life in a very dramatic fashion, and usually can be found playing the leading role in its own personal soap opera. It is very concerned with the world's problems and often feels it knows what would be best for everyone. It has incredibly high ideals of how it *should* live its life, and what others *could do* that would make their lives more perfect. If the 9 could wave a magic wand over everyone to solve all the problems and patch up all the bruised egos and cut knees, it would gladly do that. It tends to play the role of father or mother of the world.

In the Past

The pattern of the past was to get completely involved with the full melodrama of life and sigh a lot over life's myriad problems, frequently telling them and retelling them to anyone who would listen. It clung to the past and used it to explain everything. It took life very personally, paying special attention to the "pains" and "heartbreaks"—sometimes to the point of completely closing its heart, deciding life was too much pain. A great example of this is found in the country and western song, "I'll never love again...." This is living death, not living life.

In the Future

9 will know how to "let go and let God." It will realize it is here completing unfinished tasks and won't take it personally when something ends or is over. Rather, 9 will celebrate that one more end is tied up and move on to the next experience. It will look a little

more to what is coming next, rather than what it is leaving behind. It will comprehend that life has been teaching it about the full drama of humans, from abject misery all the way to total, ecstatic joy and everything that comes in between, so it can develop a higher degree of compassion and tolerance. It will savor the great value to be found in its high awareness of the beautiful in life, and will gratefully share that more freely with others. Acknowledging pain, grief, misery, and poverty as conditions of this planet, as well as joy, love, friendship, and beauty.

Conflicts With Other Numbers

Conflict generally comes from the 9 wanting to show everyone else a *better way* — sometimes referred to as "sticking its nose in everyone's business." Also, others can get a little weary of the volumes of problems a 9 can accumulate to worry about. 9 really does know what everyone else could be doing better, yet can avoid problems by allowing everyone to solve things in their own way.

Lessons to be Learned
- To accept people and conditions just as they are; to forgive, forget, and let go.
- To keep focused on *love* being the most important thing and watch as everything else drops away; to fully enjoy the art, music, culture and refinement; and to open its heart to all people, regardless of age, race, color, or any other label that can be used to separate us.
- To learn about the kinship of people-kind so that it can hold in its heart the dream of us making it work here together, one people under God, indivisible, with liberty and justice for all.
- Most of all, it's learning that its most valuable asset is a heart filled with enough love to melt any resistance it encounters. 9's lessons fall anywhere within the full gamut from deepest pain to greatest joy so that it can achieve the vast understanding and wisdom necessary to truly be able to assist others.
- And finally, it is learning to love and forgive itself.

People Skills You Might Want to Develop

Take any workshops, trainings, or seminars that will allow you to experience the immensity of your loving heart. You are an old soul on the planet, here now to help. You've prepared many life-times for this. There is nothing that you must do or say, you only need to hold acceptance and love in your heart as you actively visualize us creating a cooperative world, filled with openess, joy, trust, and love, and work on forgiving.

Where Your Talents Lie

Your talents lie in spiritual, philosophical, dramatic, musical, artistic pursuits, serving professions, or anyplace where you can in-spire, lift, and encourage the best from others.

If You Have a 9 Birthpath

Your life lesson is to forgive, love, and accept yourself just as your are, right now. Yours is the path to completion. You are finish-ing something you may have been working on for many lifetimes. People, places, and things may come into your life and be gone just as you think something new is beginning. Attribute that to the fact that there was something you needed to complete, with love. Don't be hard on yourself when this happens. Bear in mind you are an old soul, winding up lifetimes. Allow yourself the same love you give so freely to others. If your response is that you don't love them so free-ly, there's *another* area of your life lesson to work on. Your lesson is to lift out of the melodrama into the love. Surely there's a lot more to talk about when the drama is going full swing, yet what the world needs now is quiet acceptance. Everyone can see all the problems; that's easy. Yet your special job is to raise the vision of us all to the beauty of a smile, a sky full of clouds, a rainbow, two lovers togeth-er, a world of vibrant colors, sweet sounds, pungent aromas, deli-cate tastes, and tender touches. The universe speaks the language of the senses; a hug or embrace conveys love without words. Ac-cording to Pythagorean concepts, sight was bestowed upon man so that we might *observe* the harmonious motions of the heavenly spheres, and thereby regulate our own internal harmony. The sense of hearing was given us for a similar purpose—as was speech.

If You Have a 9 Destiny

If your Fairy Godmother had tapped you on the forehead with her magic wand and said, "Dear one, perceive love through all your senses, and let it emanate from you in return," your feet would have been set along the correct path. You are here to demonstrate and teach love. Give everyone the benefit of doubt and *assume* they are interacting from a place of love. Somewhere back in time, when we first read our contracts and picked the roles we would play out for each other in this incarnation, all agreements were made with a loving desire to be of assistance in whatever way would be most perfect for our highest growth and development. No matter how harsh your experience may have appeared at the time, it has contributed to your wisdom and maturity now. We are the sum total of all of our past experiences, including other lifetimes. You are an old soul finishing things up, going home to the heart of God. Learn to value life and hold it as loosely as you would a precious bird. You chose to experience this life in its depth of intensity so that you could fully understand every aspect, from all vantage points. If you were to stand outside yourself and see what you have accomplished, you would have the utmost admiration for you. You are the flower in full bloom; learn to cherish yourself and accept the admiration of those around you. If you observe strangers thinking they know you, they do. They are people you assisted with loving acts and deeds many long times ago. Karma works with good returned for good as well as bad returned for bad. Now, they recognize you and want to return some of the goodness. Your job is to accept and say thank you. You owe them nothing—you've paid in advance.

Your Heart's Desire

Your heart's desire is for beauty and love. The 9 has the biggest heart of any number, and to have this for a "heart number" can easily mean there has been lots of pain in your heart. The lessons of compassion only come through life experiences, not through TV, movies, or books. If you close your heart to protect yourself, you are closing off life itself. I'm not sure where we got the idea that pain is wrong. Maybe it came from well-meaning mommys and daddys telling us "don't do that or you'll get hurt." On this planet we have duality; all things have equal opposites. Attempting to live a life with no pain is attempting to live *half* a life. If you shut out the pain, you can easily shut out the joys and miss some of life's beautiful moments. Your heart is happiest when surrounded by beauty; seek it out and share it with others.

Pinnacle

The 9 pinnacle is a pinnacle of greatness and power. A time of intensity which brings with it a greater awareness and appreciation of life and love and beauty in the world. A time to demonstrate extreme compassion for humankind in all its suffering, ignorance and pain, especially yourself; forgiveness and acceptance start with you. Continually give yourself a break and be extra loving and supportive to yourself. There may be a great tendency on your part to try to save or fix everyone you love. However, the highest service is to hold in your loving thoughts the knowledge that they will come up with their own answers (remember, this is their experience to learn, not yours). What you can do is share your sense of beauty and harmony, and focus on the beauty instead of the pain. You can serve mankind by bringing more joy, more laughter, more forgiveness and understanding, more music, more color into the world. You will be continually faced with the choice for more drama of life or more love. It's easy to get caught up in the drama, there is so much to share there. Some of us love a good cry. I heard once that God loved good stories, so he created us as storytellers, and I suspect there's some truth in that. Yet, the most wonderful story, and the one that needs to be told most often these days, is one of creating us all into *one* family of mankind. Maybe it's the pain that bonds us. Emphasize the unity and oneness of us. 9 is a number of completions and requires that you "let go and let God" so that you can move into a higher, less personal love and understanding. The rewards are rich and filled with the goodness and joys of life once you "get" that life is not to be taken any more personally than you would an exam or pop quiz. Our goal is really graduation, and 9 brings forward those perfect things to assist with that goal.

Challenge

The 9 is probably the biggest of all challenges, because it includes the fullness of life. The challenge is to be forgiving, loving, accepting, and to learn compassion and tolerance, and requires an open, unconditional heart. The lessons learned here are mostly taught through experience, and you can choose tears and pain or great joy and laughter. The purpose of this challenge is to expand your heart with compassion enough to include all of mankind. It may offer lots of opportunities for completing karma with friends and lovers from your past—even other lifetimes. Forgiveness and understanding are the keys to opening the door of your heart. Once you've opened it to someone, they will always be in there. Since 9 is a very dramatic (melodramatic) number, the lessons look very similar to operettas or little novels. When Shakespeare said all the world is a stage, he definitely had the 9 in mind. It is really challenging you to have a great appreciation of the beauty of life, to see it in anything, including poverty and misery. This can be a time of completions and endings during which friends die, jobs end, things finish. As you learn to handle it with grace and compassion, you'll see the beauty and perfection to a system which is far grander than anything you or I could come up with, for sure. Loosen your grip on life. "Let go, and let God."

Home play: Look at your life as if it were a fairy tale or Broadway play. Have some fun with this and put in the full melodrama. Write it down and ask a good friend to read it to you while everyone shouts "author, author," and throw flowers on the stage for the successful drama you have created! Give yourself big applause and a big hug for living through it.

Attainment

9 is to achieve a life filled with beauty, love, and happiness. What you have to offer is a loving heart and the great understanding it has taken you a lifetime to accumulate. Whatever your life has been, it has opened doors to you of vast knowledge into people and the ways of the world. Share that knowledge with the tenderness and insight that come from being able to put yourself into another's place.

Law of Opposites

Pythagoras' fundamental law: Good and evil.

Words That Total 9

Love, dance, play, grow. In the alphabet, I = 9, R = 18; both reduce to 9.

Note: Some Numerologists expect a letter to be added to the alphabet when our lives are exhibiting more compassion and forgiveness.

ℵ

ℵ

The

Even

Numbers

2   4   6   8   0

Even numbers represent things of form and structure (the tangibles). They like to conform and fit in. They prefer life to go smoothly, and don't like the unexpected.

ℵ

2

Key Word

2's key word is *cooperation*. It is the partner to 1; its strength is its gentleness. It radiates the colors of gold and salmon and sings the musical note of C#. Its symbol is ∧ or +. 2 Has no special gemstone or flower. Its mineral is gold. I suspect because of its sensitivity, it vibrates with all things rather than special ones.

Attributes

2 represents the force that literally puts "two and two together." It harmonizes, soothes, negotiates, arbitrates, balances, translates, and mediates. It is patient, kind, considerate, thoughtful, gentle, supportive, and a team person. 2 is precise with details, collecting, and assembling tiny pieces. It is the number of duality.

Usual Tendencies of Behavior

It's not as easy to see a 2 as it is a 1; 2's frequently try to be invisible and are often in the background, blending in. The energy is very sensitive and intuitive. Wanting harmony at any cost, it will do the little things that need to be done for things to run smoothly. It has great abilities to take on others' characteristics, like a mime or an actor, wearing two faces. It can be very unassuming and self-depreciating, feeling it has nothing to contribute. 2 can exhibit great patience and strength, yet has the general tendency to belittle itself and not see the beauty it is or the contribution it makes. This is the number of the Age of Aquarius, and represents people coming together in harmony to cooperate, be sensitive, gentle, and thoughtful with each other. 2 is the number assisting us to create a world in which we can all work together, with no fear of speaking out because we realize clear communication is the path to understanding each other.

In the Past

2 avoided confrontation. Its desire for harmony led it into being dishonest about its feelings, saying things like "I don't know," or

"I don't care," or "It doesn't matter to me." These messages were actually saying, "I don't want to get clear on these issues as it will probably start an argument." The 2 has been a number representing lots of fears and apprehensions. There is a tendency to be afraid of its own shadow; also a tendnecy towards easily hurt feelings. 2 blows things out of proportion; it collects and holds on to hurt and pain. 2 has a strong ability to get caught up in the little details of something and forget there is a bigger picture. It frequently puts itself down as not being as intellectual as other numbers. Its strength comes from its intuition, not its intellect. The process of translating feelings into words requires great patience. This number represents someone who can walk away mumbling, "What I should have told them was...," or is afraid to say its feelings at all because it doesn't want to start an argument.

In the Future
2 will represent the peacemaker, the arbitrator or negotiator, someone who is assisting the world to come together in peace and harmony. It will see the great value that comes with the ability to soothe over hurt feelings and translate one person to another. Christ said, "Blessed are the peacemakers for they shall be called the sons of God," and also, "Blessed are the meek for they shall inherit the earth." Both of these are represented by the 2. Attributes that were long seen as unimportant, will be of great value.

Conflicts With Other Numbers
Conflict with other numbers is not really a big problem with 2. Its only trouble is when it keeps things to itself that need to be released. 2 frequently waits for the right time to discuss something and then keeps waiting and waiting, bottling things up until its stack blows, and then people say, "Oh, is that all that was bothering you?" Other numbers may have problems with the 2 because they feel the 2 is insincere, insecure, or too humble.

Lessons to be Learned
• To know the difference between avoidance and tactfulness.
• To say what it thinks.

•To remember other numbers don't get their feelings hurt as easily as the 2, that saying to itself "I know this will hurt them, so I won't say it" is really a manipulation, not giving the other number (or person) the opportunity to choose their response.

People Skills You Might Want to Develop

As the 2 learns to say its own feelings, it can then assist others to do the same thing. Few of us have perfect communication skills; we're all in the process of learning. 2 has a very valuable role to play in the future that can only be developed with experience. Take each opportunity to try speaking the whole truth. If you get a result you don't like, try another approach. Call on yourself to be resourceful; try many means to communicate your point of view and convey your feelings. Letters and telephones may be helpful as you tend to read faces for approval, without validating your perception. You might be misreading, however. When you look for disapproval, that's what you usually find.

Talents

Your talents are in the line of anything that takes patience, you have lots of that. Abilities to collect, sort through, assemble, and put together are your strengths. You are moderate in your tastes and very rhythmical. You could easily work in any of these fields: translator, actor, dancer, musician, or detail person.

If You Have a 2 Birthpath

Your life lesson is to assist others in carrying out their ideas. To learn patience, timing, and to comprehend that your strength comes from your intuition and sensitivity. 2 has a great capacity to look to others for comparison; it's fine to look, not so fine to decide others are better or smarter or that their way is superior to yours. 2 is the number that is always asking other's opinions and wanting their advice. Learn to follow your intuition. That first little voice that speaks inside you, is the one. When you argue or contradict it, it doesn't work. 2 is learning to feel its way slowly through life, bringing 2 and 2 together as you go. This frequently takes time and patience. There actually is a right and perfect time for everything, and 2 is learning to use its intuition to act at that time. This could mean sometimes you do things too soon and sometimes too late. However, the time will come when you hit it right on. Act on your intuition and validate it—you can only learn to trust yourself by trying. Don't be afraid to make mistakes; you didn't learn to walk overnight, either. You are learning to surrender to the will of God.

If You Have a 2 Destiny

If your Fairy Godmother had tapped you on the forehead with her wand and said, "Be patient with yourself while you gently unfold into life...rely on your intuition as radar," your feet would have been pointed along the correct path. You are here as a peacemaker and balancer in life. Learn what keeps you in balance, and do those things so that your life runs harmoniously. Your touch will always be a gentle one; you have the strength of water continuing to seek a different approach after its course has been blocked (while 1 rushes ahead and knocks down whatever stands in its path). This is the problem of comparing yourself to others. See what they do, listen to their words, and then take your time and follow what feels right to you.

Heart's Desire

Your heart's desire is peace, harmony, and balance in all things. You are a gentle, sensitive soul who will smooth all the ruffled feathers and do whatever is necessary to achieve tranquility. You might tend to appear timid and shy, characteristics that frequently seem undesirable. Value them, as they allow you to feel what is going on with others, and assist in your role of peacemaker. Work through your fears so that you can take your rightful place in the new world we are now creating. It's important to know what you think, feel, and want, before you can decide it doesn't matter. Learn the difference between a truce, a compromise, and actual peace. And also come into the awareness that divine order can seldom come into being without divine chaos being the prior condition.

Pinnacle

The 2 pinnacle is a time for you to move into more grace and harmony with all life. Demonstrate your abilities to adapt and flow with things. You are probably more intuitive and sensitive than ever before. The other side of that might look like you cry more easily and doubt yourself frequently. They're all really fine. Your inner strength is not really the issue here—you have plenty of it, you are becoming more supple and fluid. Use water often—it soothes, cleanses, and replenishes you. Bathe in it, drink it, listen to it, wash your hands frequently, or picture yourself being showered when you feel tired and need to refresh your energies and cleanse away the negativity you feel from others. Whatever your sex, allow yourself to become more feminine. Be gentle and loving. You may feel like you know nothing, that others know much more and you have nothing to contribute. However, contributing gentleness and sensitivity are incredibly important. You will notice people appreciate your presence even when you have nothing to say.

Challenge

The challenge of the 2: Expect to be in positions where harmony, cooperation, tact, diplomacy will be required. 2 has a great desire for peace, so your challenge is to handle things tactfully, learning the skills of an arbitrator and negotiator; you'll need to be the one who pours oil on the troubled waters, who soothes rather than agitates. This is not running away from confrontation, it is developing new skills; there really is a big difference. This is one of the most important challenges of our times; few of us have experience in saying our feelings without expecting an argument. This challenge is to put your own feelings into words and express them, and then assist others in doing the same thing. Hold on to your desire for a world of peace and harmony. Others will step forward to create that world with you. It will be a world where everyone wins. Rather than competition, we'll have cooperation. "The meek" can demonstrate this with the gentleness and sensitivity necessary to becoming role models for everyone. Approach your 2 challenge with great PATIENCE, as you are also learning to surrender. While the 1's challenge was to get clear on what you want and how to achieve it, the challenge of the 2 is to let go of it if it's not for the highest good of all concerned. This is a very soft number and teaches feminine things—to be flowing, sensitive, intuitive, tender, and gentle. All these attributes will become more and more impor- tant as we move closer to the year 2000. Two is a challenge of partnerships—on all levels.

Home play. Take the phrases, "I don't know," "It doesn't matter," or "It's not important to me," out of your vocabulary. Take each opportunity offered to know what you *do* want.

Attainment

2 is to achieve the grace of patience and the gifts of tactful communication. It is to develop your sensory systems so you live in harmony with the rhythms and flows of life. This may indicate suc- cessful partnerships in later life. Guard against feeling you have nothing to contribute.

Law of Opposites

Pythagoras' fundamental law: Odd and Even. 2 represents the Moon, is considered feminine, the right hemisphere, feelings.

Words That Total 2

Logic, cross, loyal, kind. In the alphabet, B = 2, K = 11 (which means it is very special), T = 20; all reduce to 2.

4

Key Word

4's key word is *construction*. 4 radiates the colors of green, blue, indigo, and emerald. 4 sings the musical note of D#; the sym- bol is a square. Gemstones and minerals are rhodochrosite, moon- stone, emerald, bloodstone, silver, mercury, and coral. The flower is fuschia.

Attributes

4's are the builders in life, establishing order and system in all they survey. 4's give us guidelines for our lives' foundations, such as appointment books, calendars, clocks, seasons, road maps, and bookkeeping systems. 2 puts 2 and 2 together; 4 organizes it. 4's have been called "the salt of the earth." They are the "pillars of the community," the backbone. 4 symbolizes great discipline, stamina, and stick-to-it-ivity, and ususally can muster up whatever it takes to get the job done efficiently and well.

Usual Tendencies of Behavior

If you want a job done, call on the 4. A 4 will methodically organize and construct it perfectly to your specifications. It likes to handle its life in the same manner. It loves boxes and neat, tidy completions. 4's are gifted at fitting little things into small places and are generally meticulous, often getting very caught up with each detail and forgetting there is a bigger picture. This can cause great frustration from time to time.

In the Past

4 is the symbol for discipline, the foundation upon which our lives are built. It materializes the formless and structureless. However, 4 got so caught up doing its job that it often became rigid, and demanded the same level of dedication from those around it. 4's thought safety and security were only obtained by hard work and organization, with wanting *everything* alphabetized and labeled.

In the Future

The 4 will have more to offer as it will be more flexible and resilient. Strength is demonstrated in the ability to roll with the punch as well as to stand strong in the face of adversity. 4 will see the importance of establishing guidelines, then tailoring them to expand and fit the occasion — it will give form that serves as a foundation, yet doesn't restrict the growth, saying "Let's try it" rather than "No, it can't be done that way."

Conflicts With Other Numbers

4 has a tendency to set things in concrete and make them a little harder than they need to be. As a result, it frequently has lots of problems, especially with all the odd numbers. The odd ones look just that way to a 4, which has a strong desire to get everything organized; the even ones offer a simple challenge. 2's meekly go

along, 6's take their responsibilities seriously and generally conform; 8 is a grown up 4, and while it certainly doesn't take orders easily from any other numbers it can appreciate what the 4 wants to accomplish. The odd numbers would all tend to say, "What do you want to do that for?" 1 wants to start things its own way, 3 wants to be playful and express, 5 wants to be free to explore, 7 wants to understand and gain wisdom. Now that we have arrived at 4, the symbol that represents form and structure, we've come to the first number that sets up conflicts easily with all of its associates and fellow numbers.

Lessons to be Learned
• To bring flexibility to all aspects of its life, its thinking as well as its doing. 4 tends to see life as restricted and narrow, following rules because they *are* rules. With great steadfastness of purpose, it lives in ruts, and toils along seldom complaining, forgetting the ruts are of its own making.
• It's important to do a job efficiently; it's also important to know your life is in your hands to experiment and try.
• To look for the exception to the rule every now and then. 4 is learning about flexible boxes, foundations and organization.

People Skills You Might Want to Develop
4's like to know the rules, so take lessons at anything you have the slightest interest in pursuing, and then realize there are many other ways to handle the same situation. Once you have someone else's method in your rulebook, it might be fun to see how many other ways you could come up with to handle the same thing. Learn to ease up on life and not be so caught up in plodding through to the end of your mission. A deviation from the original blueprint may very well enhance the project and make it better. Accept that everyone will have a different system and all may be valuable.

Talents
Any field that calls for dedication, persistence, and endurance is your area. That can be construction, design, mathematics, bookkeeping, farming, drafting, problem solving, anything that requires

close attention to the details from beginning to end, can use the 4's abilities.

If You Have a 4 Birthpath

Your life lesson is to be organized, dependable, punctual, efficient, and a good manager. You are learning about the foundations upon which life is built. This is the lesson of practicality, perseverance, and organization. Learn to do those things so you understand the process. Give form to things without becoming stuck in it. You are actually learning to be down-to-earth and practical so that you can assist others to give form to the things they do. There's a big difference between having *an idea* of something wonderful that could work and *doing it*. The 4 symbolizes the *doers* in life; every time you accomplish a goal you have set for yourself, stop and acknowledge it. Goal accomplishing is as simple as planning to have company over for dinner, organizing the menu, shopping, cooking, and eating. You do that all the time. Carry that into all aspects of your life and see the importance of routine. Everything you do in your life is constructed on the foundations you lay down, so pay attention.

If You Have a 4 Destiny

If your Fairy Godmother touched your forehead at birth with her magic wand and said, "Raise your eyes to the skies as you labor to construct the strong foundation that will support heaven on earth," your feet would have been pointed along the correct path in life. You are here as an organizer to give substance to things. Your contributions will be of a very practical nature. Years ago, I took part in the drumming of an all-night Indian dance. I noticed that any time my drumbeat faltered, the dancers were affected. Through that experience, I came to value the 4 for its steadiness. We may take it for granted, like the rhythm of our heartbeat, but as soon as it falters, everything is thrown off. You have a fine gift of steadiness; allow others their special gifts and realize it takes us all to make up the whole. You have great stamina and endurance. However, don't treat yourself as if you were a robot. Life is about living. If you see yourself adversely affected by all the changes that are coming more frequently now, reassure yourself with the knowledge that divine chaos comes before divine order, and that a new form is coming forward. What you are wanting to hold onto, was built on a foundation of shifting sands. The new order will be established on a firmer structure.

Heart's Desire

Your heart lies in creating an organized, orderly world where everything runs efficiently and nothing ever gets misfiled. You love symmetry and balance. This can sometimes be a mixed blessing, as few things stay in their proper filing drawer these days. When God was handing out the instructions and "how-to" booklets, you were the one who volunteered to supervise the work. Sometimes you take this job a little too seriously, forgetting that true strength is achieved through a balance of hard and soft. Earthquakes destroy buildings because they are inflexible and can't bend. You have great stamina and fortitude, and can accomplish anything to which you set your heart. The world can greatly benefit from these strengths, and you can benefit from becoming more pliant and adaptable.

Pinnacle

The 4 pinnacle: 'discipline' may be a word you frequently hear inside. Use it with great tenderness and consideration; inner strength is a blessing. This can be a hard working period that you'll look back upon with satisfaction for your accomplishments, although at times you may feel frustrated and repressed. No one is really holding you back; you are being asked to demonstrate your understanding of rules, regulations, appointments, rows, columns, efficiency, etc. Planet Earth runs on these things. Can you imagine our life without organization and planning? What if all the traffic lights turned green at once (or red)? While this period may feel difficult, keep remembering you are a human being...*not* a human doing; demonstrate your knowledge of practicality.

Challenge

The challenge of the 4 is to learn about and understand the laws, foundations, and structures. On some level, it is teaching you how to live in a box, with great understanding of walls, well-fitting joints, and mitered corners. Learn to be methodical, well organized, and dedicated to completions. It is a challenge to be down-to-earth and practical. This period may feel restrictive, and it is. Learn what you can about living with restrictions. Give it full attention and learn this challenge well, as it represents the very guidelines and structures on which this planet operates. Every time you demonstrate punctuality, efficiency, organizational skills, commend yourself and appreciate the importance of the practical work you are doing. Yet, don't get so caught up in the structure and organization that you lose your flexibility. You are learning to organize well—for the experience—not to set it in concrete and have it stay that way forever.

Home play: To be done anywhere it's needed. Organize a bookcase alphabetically or by subject; clean out two drawers in your desk or dresser, straighten a closet or part of the garage or some area that you avoid looking at because it appears too disorganized. Take yourself out to dinner to celebrate.

Attainment
4 is to value the benefits that come with self-discipline and bringing a practical viewpoint into all matters. It is to appreciate the need for order and have the skills to accomplish it. This may indicate you have some work ahead of you; "retirement" may become one of your private jokes. Guard against getting too set in your ways.

Law of Opposites
Pythagoras' fundamental law of opposites: Right and Left.

Words That Total 4
Yes, work, safe, unicorn. In the alphabet, D = 4, M = 13, V = 22; all reduce to 4.

6

6 is special in many ways. One unusual characteristic is that while it is obviously an even number, it also has a unique relationship with 3 and 9—called a triad. 3, 6, and 9 all represent different levels of love, beauty, service. 3 is symbolized by a triangle; 6 is symbolized by 2 triangles, (also recognized as the Star of David, or a six-pointed star); and 9 is symbolized by 3 triangles. 6 represents love; romantic love, tender, affectionate, benevolent, passionate love. The love of people for each other, which leads to relationships, families creating nests, building homes; patriotic love, which leads to service of country; devotion and concern for people, which leads to social welfare and reform programs. Since 6 is probably the most misunderstood of all the energies, it's not too surprising that some of us are only now starting to recognize, appreciate, and experience *love*.

Key Word

The key word for 6 is *loving service*. It radiates the colors of peach, scarlet, and heliotrope. It sings the musical note of F. There are many gemstones and minerals that vibrate with 6: jasper, onyx, topaz, Herkimer diamond, and citrine. The flowers are tulips, mistletoe, laurel and chrysanthemums. The symbols are the hexagon, cube, and six-pointed star.

Attributes

Loyalty, idealism, responsibility, devotion, service, great love of beauty, social awareness, conscientiousness, truthfulness, and virtue are attributes of 6.

Usual Tendencies of Behavior

For centuries and lifetimes, 6 has taken care of us. It has nursed us, nurtured us, loved and supported us on all levels— emotionally, physically, mentally, spiritually, and financially. It tends to put everyone ahead of itself and be the long-suffering martyr. This is the vibration that maintains the traditional standards, setting up rules and mores for the family and community to abide by. It tends to watch everyone with a caring eye to make sure they are all doing the "right" thing, and has a strong tendency to feel *guilty* about almost everything.

In the Past

6 personified "love thy neighbor as thyself." It felt the more it did for others, the more love it would be demonstrating. The problem was, it had no sense of what "love for *itself*" meant, and assumed that came from others being so grateful and appreciative for all the good work performed. That translates to the 6 always looking outside itself for approval and gratitude. On more than one occasion it felt victimized. It frequently was incredibly thoughtful of others' needs and wants, and supplied them without being asked or invited. Sometimes this built up huge resentments on the part of the "doer" as well as the "doee." 6 was the number always praised for being mature, responsible, and dependable as a child, who grew up expecting to get *strokes* for demonstrating those same characteristics. It still wanted to be "mother's or daddy's big girl or boy," often forgetting to have any joy or fun in its life (as a grown-up 3 needs to). It thought service was for the rewards reaped, which led to lots of resentments when those rewards were not forth-coming. 6 had a great tendency towards guilt feelings, that come from not "doing enough," and could be recognized by the frequency with which it said "should" or "ought to." It also could be recognized as being the "perfect example" and wanting to play "perfect roles" of mother, daughter, son, boss, employee, lover, friend, whatever, commonly not realizing its job was *just to love*. 6 had an especially fine sense and appreciation of the beautiful, which it commonly put down as *unimportant*.

In the Future

6 will comprehend that if it has a loving relationship with itself, it then has so much more to share with others and so will do those things to accomplish this. It will know that if it gives a little bit of itself to lots of people, no one will have much. However, if it keeps it all, and enhances it with love and appreciation, everyone will

benefit. A heart overflowing with love, is a joyful experience in which everyone can participate. The most important service is to share the abundance of love.

The future 6 will be a friend to itself and be loyal, sensitive, tender, kind, considerate and thoughtful—to itself. Achieving this, it will choose to have the joy in its life that comes from service. It will not be concerned with how it looks to others, nor have much charge on doing things "right," knowing a free expression of service from a loving heart is always perfect. It will have a good self-image, be its own best friend, and know that sometimes agreeing to shoulder full responsibility, hinders rather than helps. It will cultivate the understanding that love can be expressed with a "No" as well as an "Okay, I'll do it." It will value its sense of beauty and share that gift more fully. Finally, it will remember that it is a "grown-up 3," and bring more laughter and humor into its life.

It seems to me that when Jesus came to Earth and spoke of love, the 6, being such a responsible number, set out to do those things that "looked like" love. For centuries it ran around trying to please everyone, hoping it had it down "right." Years ago, a friend and I spent several months puzzling over the question, "How do people know we love them if we don't *do anything* for them?" I finally concluded love is a condition of the heart, requiring constant acceptance of what is, lots of humor, and continual forgiveness. It also requires me to feel confident and secure enough inside myself to perceive love in all things, in all ways.

Conflicts With Other Numbers

6 has stronger conflicts with the odd numbers than any number we've met up to this point. Primarily due to the fact that 6 feels so *responsible* for everyone's thoughts, words, and deeds. It wants to fix everything for everyone, and has a tendency to lay "guilt trips" on others. On its negative side, 6 can exemplify the concept of "big brother watching." 1 would not tolerate someone looking over its shoulder, wanting to mother it, or tell it what to do for its own good. 2 would probably appreciate the concern and be glad to assist 6 in any way. In fact, of all the numbers, 2 probably has the greatest ability to perceive that 6 is coming from loving concern rather than just being "bossy" or meddlesome. 3 would laugh

and go its own way. 4 would get down to work and efficiently organize the service project that 6 has in mind. 5 would go on strike and rebel against whatever the 6 suggests it "should" be doing. 7 would retreat inside and hide, pretending it doesn't hear or is too involved to participate in the plan of the 6. 8 would turn around and direct the actions of the 6, and 9 would accept it and see it is trying to do loving actions, that frequently get mistaken for "do-gooding."

Lessons to be Learned

6's lesson has far-reaching consequences as it's all about love: what love looks like, acts like, sounds like, and is. Stop a moment and picture a world without love, then picture a world enfolded in love. 6 is assisting to create the latter, not based on theory, rather on experience and deep knowledge. 6 can only teach what it knows. A key: is complete self-acceptance and appreciation, now. Just look at your life with the eyes of a stranger and see all the loving, generous, thoughtful things you constantly do.

•Take time to value yourself. If there is stress in a situation, don't do more! Go get a massage or do domething really nuturing for yourself, and you'll be amazed how different things will look.
•To learn about relationships and responsibility. Take this seriously and understand the primary one is with *yourself*.
•Take all the "shoulds" out of your vocabulary.

People Skills You Might Want to Develop

Learn how to allow others to assist you — and realize their assistance is coming from love. There is a fine art to *receiving* and saying "Thank you." Practice it. Take any training, class, or seminar that is about love, acceptance or forgiveness, and develop your artistic abilities, even though you may not think you have any. Be aware of your tendency to teach as well as your tendency of saying "You" when you really mean "I." Every time you say "I," you're claiming your power; any time you say "You," you're confusing things.

Talents

Your talents lie in any fields and area where a responsible person is needed. Your deep sense of beauty and service make you valuable in many walks of life. From banker, to interior designer, nurse, social worker, police, flight attendant, anyplace where you add to the beauty, harmony, and education. Look for a place where you have the opportunity to laugh and express the loving in your heart.

If You Have a 6 Birthpath

The life lesson is about relationships, repsonsibility, service, and love. Considered the number representing marriage and divorce, it's commonly involved in one of these endeavors. Remember, 6 is learning about love, not demonstrating proficiency. 6 expects all its "roles" to be played *perfectly*. It frequently has a hard time handling divorce, and sees it as a failure. If it is learning about relationships, it would follow that each relationship would offer a challenge. As 6 puts others' approval ahead of its own and tries so hard to do "the right thing" for everyone, it frequently feels itself a victim. All lessons are structured to teach you how to be in a good relationship with yourself. If the 6 pleases itself, that's at least one person well-satisfied. Strange as it may seem, it is your service to others to take good care of *yourself*. What a wonderful world this will be when everyone is fully responsible for their own happiness, health, creativity, and joy. As you respect yourself, others will respect you also. You are a server, not a servant. Bless the family and community with the loving essence that is you.

If You Have a 6 Destiny

If your Fairy Godmother had touched your forehead at birth with her magic wand, saying "Treasure yourself...you are a beautiful expression of God's love...your responsibility is to share that love joyfully," your feet would have been pointed along the correct path in life.

You are here demonstrating love in all things. Responsibility feels very heavy when there is neither love nor laughter involved. Ask yourself why you are doing it, if you are not enjoying it. The most valid answer would be, "Because I want to." This puts you in the position of being responsible for your own life—any other answer tends to put you into the victim role. I was amazed to realize that "No" equals 11 (the spiritual teacher). When I teach classes, we start with everyone going to the blackboard to write numbers, while they try to feel of the vibrations by looking at them. Everyone writes 1's , then 2's, then 3's, 4's, and so on. Each time I say, "If you had never seen that symbol before, what would it look like to you?" Once a whole class went up to the board and wrote 6's. When I asked what they saw there, they all said "Bubbles!" It made me realize that responsibility is as heavy as I make it.

Avoid "should-ing on yourself." I have an idea that in times to come, mothers will wash their children's mouths out for using the word "should!" Bring the color and joy of life into each interaction; you are here to enjoy all of life's blessings: good books, food, friends, art, music, culture, the finest things of life. Demonstrate your loving expression through everything, in all ways.

Heart's Desire

Your heart's desire is to bring the romance of life into all you do. Your heart lies in the beautiful, and it's important to surround yourself with beauty. Home is a necessary ingredient in your life. When you travel, take something that says "home" with you to make you more comfortable. Learn to adapt your surroundings to be harmonious, as you draw nourishment from them. You are here nourishing others, make sure to nourish yourself well so that you can fulfill your job. Just like a bank account, it's important to make deposits so that you can make withdrawals. You have a strong desire to fix and repair everyone; start with yourself. A dear friend once remarked, "Life is a process of continually recovering." Allow each person their own process, and don't take more on your shoulders than you are comfortable with. Your desire is to nurse, teach, lift, and support. Do that from a loving place that empowers each person—teaching them to fish rather than feeding them.

Pinnacle

The 6 pinnacle: This is a time to demonstrate service as a loving *gift* more than a responsibility. It may be necessary to move out of any remaining victim consciousness and realize you are free to choose your *outlook* on life as well as your actions. You are the server, not the servant. If you respect yourself and what you have to offer, others will cherish it more. You bring beauty with you.

Add more color, smells, sounds, flowers to your life. Love comes in many forms. Part of your service is to *be* love and beauty—not *do* love and beauty. Family, home, and civic duties can be very important to you in this cycle. Demonstrate their importance by making adjustments so that everyone is carrying their fair share. If you're doing it all yourself—STOP!—and see what happens. Forsake the path of reaction, and choose love.

Challenge

The challenge of the 6 is for you to become your best friend. Learn to do all the things for yourself that you would do for others. Be loving, kind, considerate, thoughtful, generous, gentle, loyal, sensitive—with yourself. This challenge brings extra responsibilities with it as you are being *challenged* to deal with life in a more loving way. Relationships are a tool for greater understanding of yourself within the framework of that relationship. They will challenge you to stay in your loving heart, while you solve problems or make adjustments. Since 6 represents marriage and divorce, these issues might naturally arise now. Love yourself through them. If you feel like a martyr, like nobody appreciates ALL the things you do, chances are you are agreeing to do things you really don't want to do and placing the resentment on *others* for asking.

Home play: Practice saying, "No, I don't want to." Buy yourself flowers, get a massage, a facial, go to a concert, or do some other wonderfully, thoughtful thing you would suggest to a friend... *listen* to your own advice and ACT on it. Take care of your health.

Attainment

6 is to feel more concerned with others. Value your time and energy and find ways to be of service that are enjoyable. This may indicate a new romance or marriage in later years. Guard against meddling or the desire to fix everyone's problems.

Law of Opposites

Pythagoras' fundamental law of opposites: Rest and Motion.

Words That Total 6

Truth, teacher, volunteer, reincarnation. In the alphabet, $F = 6$, $0 = 15$, $X = 24$; all reduce to 6

8

Key Words

Balance of the material and spiritual. 8 radiates the colors of canary and mauve. It sings the musical note of G, and the symbol is the scales of balance and ⟨⟩ Gemstones and minerals are chrysolite, sardonix, calcite, and mica. The flowers are begonias, jasmine, bluebells, dahlias, and rhododendron.

Attributes

The name GOD totals to 8. It is the number of mastery. Its desire is to master the material world, i.e., earth, and bring that into balance with heaven. 8 symbolizes the law and is expressed through the law of retribution: for every action, there is an equal and opposite reaction; and through the law of karma, or cause and effect; "as above, so below," and "an eye for an eye." It further represents the law brought by Moses, which is the commandments and all the "Thy shall nots," as well as the new commandment of Jesus, "Love each other just as much as I love you." 8 is a grown-up 4 and wants to organize and structure the laws that govern the world. It drives itself constantly to do better and has high expectations of perfection. It generally has a finely attuned sense of right from wrong, and an active conscience or lack of one.

Usual Tendencies of Behavior

Of all the numbers, the 8 is the one that is changing most with the times (since the '80s). 8 has been known to symbolize success, money, power, and achievement in the world. It tended to be masculine, forceful energy, wanting to manifest and demonstrate great mastery of the physical world. Success and achievement were measured by the large amounts of money and possessions acquired. It's difficult to say usual tendencies of the 8, as even as I write this, the balance of power is shifting. The law the 8 created and maintained rested on the foundation of there being a straight and narrow path of rightness and wrongness. People were advised to think about their errors and mistakes to make sure they never made them again. We see now that if you dwell on something, it's sure to happen. A God of great fear was easily created by somebody "out there" who knew what was right for us and dictated the behavior to which we either measured up or beat ourselves over the head if we didn't or couldn't. 8 tends to appear as if it knows everything and often will deny itself new experiences and stifle its urges for expansion and growth rather than be seen looking unequal and unsure of itself.

Pattern of the Past

As the 8 represents balance, it also represented unbalance, and frequently stayed in the negative side of things rather than moving freely, back and forth, from side to side, positive, negative. One of the 8's roles is judge, which it took as permission to weigh and evaluate other people's actions, thoughts, and words. Commonly, if it had learned to ease up on others it still could be *its own* worst enemy and measure itself with incredibly high standards. 8 was the work-a-holic, wanting to accumulate all the prosperity symbols of the material world and sometimes be willing to do almost anything to accomplish those goals. It felt this to be the true measure of success. It commonly was represented by people with a desire for vast material wealth or those on the other side of the pendulum who were trying to convince themselves and others that money had no real importance in life, neither side being a balanced approach. 8's were easy to spot as the directors, controllers, and manipulators in life, frequently arguing and shouting that they were right (and others were wrong), having the transitory joys of more and more *things* money could buy. The 8 of the past frequently associated itself with the negative patterns of life— freely pointing out others' mistakes to them; calling right and wrong from their own personal value system; being people who lived their lives outside of the law or judiciously; and sometimes, self-righteously, inside it.

In the Future

8, being the number that represents balance, will be able to demonstrate the inner poise that is the result of balanced hemispheres of the brain, masculine and feminine energies, as well a balanced head and heart. Instead of looking to judge right from wrong, it will be firmly committed to monitoring itself to see when it goes out of balance so it can immediately take those steps that center it firmly back in the middle. Being aware that it represents great power and authority, it will turn that over to a higher authority and will fully integrate God into all things. It will be very aware of the consequences that come as a result of each of its actions, and fully comprehend the manner in which it creates its *own* reality so that it can be a joyful co-creator with God. 8's job is to follow the path outlined to it: going up to heaven, getting what it needs, and returning to integrate that back into the earth. It does this into infinity. It will know that it no longer needs to force, strain, and manipulate to get to the top, having learned that just by breathing and relaxing, it can accomplish the same things with more joy. It will have a deeper understanding of cosmic law and so be better equipped to assist our lawmakers into integrating man's law with God's law. It will understand that real wealth and true happiness come from seeking the Kingdom of God, first.

Conflicts With Other Numbers

Conflicts with other numbers are great, especially the odd numbers. As the 8 represents power and authority, it frequently exercises that at every opportunity. The 8 as a young person is often rebellious with a deep need to prove to everyone and anyone that its way is the "right" way—often not realizing that everyone's way has some truth in it for them. Even as an older person, the 8 sometimes fails to realize that as it truly is right, others will know that in the long run without having anything "proved" to them. Commonly, the 8 feels called upon to judge and critize others' actions, and even when it's not, it can be so judgemental of itself that others feel that, and assume they're being judged, too. The 1 and 8 are very similar in energy, each wanting things to be done their way, they frequently compete with each other for power. This can be particularly true with a woman expressing 1 and a man expressing 8. She may feel the need to work extra hard to assert herself in a masculine world and will easily cast him in the role of an authority figure or see him as a threat (whether he *is* or not). 2 will go along, unless the 8 is being so tactless and bossy that the 2 starts to build up resentments, which could lead to it doing some acts of passive aggression. 3 could choose to laugh the 8 away or even find a pleasant way to get around it. 4's and 8's can be very harmonious and an unbeatable team for accomplishment as long as they both want the same things; also, both can be very stubborn and set in their ways. 5's approach to anything unpleasant is to look for an avenue of escape. 6 is such a loving, responsible energy it would get right in there and pitch a hand (or feel guilty for not). 7's would distance themselves.

An interesting dynamic sometimes occurs between two 8's in that one often just assumes the other is being critical and judgemental, and acts (or reacts) accordingly. Also, 8 projects like a "father figure," and that draws all sorts of reactions. Some feel the need to "prove themselves better" (like the old gunslinger who gets gunned down in the saloon by some young upstart who recognized his name and reputation), others looking for approval. 9's have the potential to admire the 8, understanding what it wants to accomplish, and hopefully support and encourage it to expand more into its heart.

Lessons to be Learned

The 8 is learning about balance, if that is the lesson, what you can know is that it's continually going from out-of-balance. Just as a pendulum has to swing back and forth to keep the clock ticking, so the 8 needs to do what it does. Yet, just a little swinging is necessary to keep going, not really a huge arc.

•To learn to use its incredible power in a more balanced fashion.

•To recognize when it is unbalanced, and do those things that will *center* it again. Staying in balance would be like bringing a see-saw to balance and expecting it to stay there. So it's not a "wrong" to go off center, it's to be expected. Just practice getting more aware, and do it quicker. When everyone around is angry and upset, look inside yourself and see what's being reflected to you.

•To take full responsibility for the repercussions of your actions. You are learning about the law of cause and effect, and that's it, in motion.

People Skills You Might Want to Develop

8's have such a strong tendency to feel they're right. If so, you don't have to prove it; it's enough that *you* know. Others will find that out without your needing to actually prove anything. Learn to relax in your "rightness" and you'll avoid lots of confrontations that you probably don't enjoy any more than anyone else. We are no longer in the times of the game called "winners and losers." Now, it's more a question of how to create a world where we'll *all* win. Put your energies into keeping harmony *inside* yourself.

Where Your Talents Lie

The world of money or law are your worlds: investments, speculations, banking. Your skills lie in directing or managing, giving form in whatever line, such as choreographer, conductor, adminsitrator, efficiency expert. You may have a particular gift in a line where brilliance is needed with strategy and knowledge of tactics. Also, you belong in the healing professions that assist people to be more balanced in body, mind, and/or spirit.

If You Have an 8 Birthpath

Your life lesson is to learn mastery *in* and *of* your life. That may mean to take control of your life, or it may mean to loosen control and bring God into more of a partnership. You are here to deal with your creations from other lifetimes and learn to take responsibility for what you're creating now. You have the potential for great accomplishments; which can either be done from your ego or from cooperation with God. One path has infinitely more power than the other; you are learning from your choices. As you breathe, focus on your breath healing and balancing you. Allow your life to happen, rather than constantly pushing it.

If You Have an 8 Destiny

If your Fairy Godmother had tapped your forehead at birth with her magic wand, saying "You are a prince of the realm, achieving balance as you go from the light into the darkness and back again; be ever vigilant and stay centered in your heart," your feet would have been pointed along the correct path. This is the path of power, authority, and recognition; of manifesting great things in the material world. It is the path of the general. It is a path that will give you many opportunities to choose between right and wrong, good and bad. 8 constantly must make the choices. One is the path of liberation, the other path called reincarnation. The 8 frequently lives a life filled with laws and structures of its own creation. Allow yourself some elbow room and space to breathe and grow; stop to smell the roses along the way. You have a very special connection with God and are here demonstrating that you are a law unto yourself. You have an understanding of things of the physical world that is very unique. Sometimes it may puzzle you that others' value systems and views are so different than yours. You are an authority; point out injustice and unfairness wherever you see them, yet do it from a balanced place inside yourself to assist in bringing about greater harmony rather than a greater degreee of separateness. Everyone now is learning to look inside themselves, and so will accept guidance only from one who is living the teachings that they preach.

Your Heart's Desire

Your heart's desire is one of great power to bring about balance and harmony on the planet. You have the energy to move heaven and earth to accomplish this. Lighten up and learn to cultivate the assistance of others who want to help. With your tendency to take over control and direct the show, it's sometimes difficult for others to share in the project. The project this time is creating a new world coalition merging countless views and opinions. You like things to be orderly and organized, and this may be a very unsettling time for you as all the values are rapidly changing. We will no longer be able to hold onto the things that were once considered important. The 8 of the past worked with trust funds; the 8 of the future will be simply working with trust.

Pinnacle

8 as a pinnacle asks you to demonstrate great knowledge of the law—on all levels. It is requiring honesty and integrity and a great drive for accomplishment on the physical plane. This can be a time of overthrowing governments and standing up clearly for what appears fair and just to you. While it's a time to seize each

opportunity to stand up for what you think is right, remember there is "rightness" in everyone. Balance can be a delicate issue, as it is so easy to lose it. You are a little see-saw that can be blown out of balance by a blast of wind—and yet, the job of the see-saw is to go up and down. In fact, it can't even go down without going up first. Apply this to your life; the desire of the period is to balance, so movement and change are a big part of the picture. There *really* is no right or wrong, good or bad; it is only your *perception* of them. Look for the grays, and do those things that will keep you centered and in balance. There is an incredible amount of drive for mastery at this time. Keep turning things over to God and stay out of your ego. Your biggest job is to breathe— deeply. The desire is to direct, control, and orchestrate everything around and inside of you. Out of balance, that can look like a disaster; done from a loving heart, it can be a great assistance and help to all. This can be a time of outstanding brilliance in the world of money, power, and authority, or a time when you take a few steps forward, followed by a few in the other direction. Look into the inner meaning of these things, and don't get caught up thinking they are the meaning of your life. *All* things come from God, our unlimited Source of supply.

Challenge

The challenge of the 8 is towards balance on all scores, on all levels. It is teaching greater understanding of karma and responsibility. Learn that if you say or do a certain thing, another thing will certainly happen as a result. This is the law of cause and effect. Observe how you create your life; stand up in your power and become an authority in your life. Money issues may be re-evaluated and balanced with Spirit, the Higher Law. Coretta King once said, "We come from the time of 'an eye for an eye,' and what did that get us but half-blind people?" This challenge is truly for fairness and justice for all—even yourself. 8 wants to "master the material plane," and may have almost a compulsion for you to "make" something of yourself that "shows" in the material world. Be merciful, fair, just, kind and considerate with yourself. Instead of being your own worst critic, become your own star supporter and do those things that keep you balanced and centered inside yourself. It may be easy to see all negatives. Challenge yourself constantly to look for the positives.

Home play: Breathe a lot. Realize balance is an ever- moving, ever-changing thing that can't be held onto any longer than you can hold onto your breath. Between the breath you take in and the breath expelled, you are in perfect balance. Spend a whole day seeing ONLY the positive side of everything, then follow that with 15 minutes each day for 30 days.

Attainment

8 is to achieve a greater sense of direction and balance in life. Practice those things that keep you in harmony so that you can stay centered wherever you are. This may indicate a career in politics or in the world of high finance. Guard against being critical and negative in your approach to things. Look for balance.

Law of Opposites

Pythagoras' fundamental law: Darkness and light.

Words that Total 8

Prosperity, think, unity, goal, rebirth. In the alphabet, H = 8, Q = 17, Z = 26; all reduce to 8.

0

0 symbolizes the whole world. When added to a digit, 0 makes it more *mature,* signifying that number has been around the whole world and returned to work on that quality from a higher perspective.

It's possible to have a 0 on one the Planes of Expression, and frequently a 0 Challenge appears.

The 0 Challenge can be a time of considerable growth and somehow offers the choice of dealing with all of the Challenges or none of them. While I have known people who choose none and took nine years off and worked only with their other numbers, most people these days are too busy maturing to have the luxury of 9 years of rest. So it turns into a crash course in humanity. Learning all at once, the Challenges others get to experience one at a time. I've been in a 0 challenge for 11 years and am almost accustomed to the fact that just as one area gets covered, another bursts its seams. At first it felt like "sock it to me" time with the Challenges coming from every direction—children, finances, car, job, relationships, etc. As a first Challenge, with the person not knowing anything else about life, it can be incredibly difficult. They're always glad to know when it will be over. A 0 Challenge can truly be the hardest time of their life. Go back and re-read all the Challenges and know that one will be completely changed and mellowed through the 0 Challenge. It's vital to rest a lot, take it easy. Just surviving entitles anyone to extra appreciation.

Home play: Try all the home play assignments, get 10 hugs daily, and acknowledge yourself for your strength. You're a real warrior!

⚜

The

Master

Numbers

These very special numbers are an area of great interest to many people, and will become more so in time. When I first started reading Numerology books, some of them made no mention of the Master Numbers, others emphasized them so strongly that people changed their names to become them, perhaps thinking it would make them more special. What I've generally found regarding these numbers is a lot of confusion. My concept is that wherever a Master Number appears, it represents a stronger dedication to assist in the evolutionary lift (the great awakening) that is presently occurring. Just as it is necessary to develop your body to be a world-class athlete, so it is necessary to endure lots of life's challenges to be strong enough to "lift" the planet. And somewhere that dedication is recorded, so that whether you remember or not, it's been made. The appearance of a Master Number reflects the wisdom and maturity necessary to have extra choices and responsibilities in life. Somehow, things seem especially complicated with a Master Number for a Birthpath or Destiny. Some of those complications develop in babyhood when we "buy into the program" that babies know nothing and those big people who surround us (who we look to as gods or the final word) know it all. On some level, each number is a Master Number and very special—doing its unique job (symbolically) in its own way. So part of the significance of these numbers can be explained by the *doubled digit* which adds extra emphasis; another part is that the 2, 4, 6, and 8 carry *seeds of greatness* within them. To get a firm understanding of this, it's necessary to start back at the roots. Just as a person is always a grown-up child, so also the 11, 22, 33, and 44 are still very much a part of their earlier selves: 2, 4, 6, and 8. People expressing these are a composite, drawing from the positive and negative sides of all the numbers involved. When compared to a single digit (which represents a single vortex of energy being developed, refined, or mastered—with a negative side and a positive), Master Numbers are more like the patterns you watch when you throw a handful of pebbles into the water—all the circles radiating out and interconnecting. So to get a full understanding of the Master Numbers, please read ALL the component parts.

Wherever you spot one of these compound digits, in any area involving the name *or* birthday, it's important to acknowledge it. Remember, it's AS IF IT WERE REDUCED, *and* AS IF IT WEREN'T, and is the EXCEPTION to the rule that numbers are always reduced down to single digits. Example: 11, when added becomes 2 (1 + 1 = 2); now, instead of reducing down the 11, it's written 11/2 and read that way, thereby taking into account all the different energies that are symbolized. We are seeing *three* energies represented: two 1's, an 11, and 2. It's important to check anything that totals 2, 4, 6, or 8 to see if a master number has been missed. For instance:

	3	(4)			3	(22/4)
	R U T H				R U T H	
	9 2 8				9 2 8	
	1				19	

I've seen it explained that if a person was living to their highest, they then expressed the Master Number; otherwise, they reverted back to the lowest potential. It seems obvious to me that very few of us live our lives to our full potential day in and day out. People flash in and out of these extremes anytime they expand into a more positive outlook. Master Numbers have a higher possibility for lifting into brilliance. Also, having the potential of a Master Number offers the opportunity for a larger, more global viewpoint. For instance, a 4 might be hard at work in the community while a 22/4 would be organizing a world-wide project like UNICEF. These strengths may be lying dormant somewhere, waiting to be awakened, and frequently this recognition serves to stir them in their hidden place.

When you spot a Master Number, always remember it's there —even if it gets lost in adding during the reducing process. Master Numbers can be used for good or evil, depending upon the free will of the person. It's like sitting on a powder keg—and has been known to explode out to benefit the world, or implode, destroying itself.

11/2

(Includes All the Qualities of Both 1 and 2)

Key Word

Spiritual teacher, visionary, peacemaker, whose desire is to illuminate the world with its vision of harmony and cooperation. Colors are violet, yellow, black, white, apricot, and the gold from 2. Gemstones are garnet and saphire; flowers are violet and camellia. The musical note is A. The guardian angel is Uriel.

Attributes

11 wants to balance the feminine and masculine energies, and in doing so, achieve, and then go on to teach balance. Great integrity, strength, and gentleness are needed. 11/2 yearns to be

both an oak tree and a willow, and can vacillate between those two or lean more strongly on one side than the other. 11's power comes from its strong intuition. Yet, it frequently isn't secure enough to believe that. It has the potential for being a great actor, easily wearing many faces. This can be scary if it doesn't know who it is underneath the facade. The two 1's say "get real clear on who you are"; the 2 says "surrender your will to the higher Will." This is what the 11/2 has to teach the world, and it can only teach from its own experience. In the future, people will be led by teachings that agree with what feels right inside themselves. Seldom does 11/2 fit into any model of what a teacher "looks like." It is teaching by what it does—not what it says. When the inner voices are contradicting each other, it's hard to decide which to follow.

11/2 needs permission to explore all of its complexities with the reminder that the angels are working alongside. When in doubt about which step to take—take little ones, but keep taking them. The 2 likes to do things slowly—the 1 likes to rush in. *Feel* your way along, is some advice to solving this problem.

The 11/2 can be confusing to others, and more so to itself. It takes great courage to "invent life"—an 11/2 is doing just that. *Speak your words so that they bring people together harmoniously.*

22/4

(Includes All the Attributes of both 2 and 4)

Key Word

Master builder, symbolizing the *architect of peace*. The colors are blue-green and gold; sings the note of A. The flowers are lily and daisy; St. Thomas is the guardian angel.

Attributes

Because of the even numbers, life for the 22/4 is more *solid* than it is for the 11/2. Things are more tangible, and accomplishments are more in the physical, therefore easier for everyone to see. This number can bring into manifestation the things 11/2 dreams about. After developing the qualities of 4, the 22 will utilize that knowledge to assist in building our world on a more secure foundation. 22/4 has a tendency to get so caught up in the big picture that it misses the details, or so involved with minutia that it gets lost in it. It's as if God presented 22/4 with a bag of building blocks and it spends all of its time putting them together. While it's working diligently to assemble them, it can be quite a while before the construction is recognizable. Many times a sense of urgency accompanies this number. It knows it's here to do something, and while it generously does that, that feeling may still persist. It takes many years to learn to run things smoothly here on this planet, and years to learn to accumulate all the knowledge and skills necessary to construct what's to be built in the end. Just as the "overnight success" who practices for 25 years before discovery, the 22/4 keeps plugging along, and its solid strength goes to structure a foundation under any of the accompanying numbers in the chart.

A big part of the development necessary with this Master Number is to focus on the attributes of the 2. Communication skills need to be finely tuned. The 22/4 has important things to say to the world—that need to be both heard and understood. Patience, tact, and diplomacy are graces. These attributes will be greatly appreciated as the world works toward global harmony.

3 3/6

(Includes All the Attributes of 3 and 6)

Key Word

Daughter/son of God. Symbolizing someone who is joyfully bringing forward the higher consciousness of love—termed the "Christ Consciousness." It vibrates with things of the 3 and the 6. The color is orange-peach, the gem is diamond, and the musical note is B. The guardian is Archangel Michael.

Attributes

The confusion with this number comes with the concept of "What is service?" Service and responsibility become joyful experiences when done from a loving heart. Its job is to speak the words of love and accentuate what 3 represents: *joy, light,* and *creativity.* The 33/6 is here to lovingly and playfully teach that life on earth can be fun.

44/8

(Includes All the Attributes of 4 and 8)

Key Word

Master balancer.

Attributes

I really know very little about this number except that its presence is starting to be felt. It is the energy that will bring a new form onto the planet. A geodesic dome is constructed of triangles —and I've heard that our planet is constructed that way also. The triangle is the strongest form, and it stands on a square base, just as the three-sided pyramid is supported by a four-sided foundation. There are four sides to our planet: north, south, east, and west, and our existence is called three-dimensional—with a fourth dimension coming soon. So somewhere our next master number, 44/8, is waiting to come forward, bringing with it the stability that comes from having God as the foundation stone.

Living the full potential of the Master Numbers (or any number) seems to be a matter of dedication and choice. That is living in its most *positive.* It might mean taking each opportunity to vigilantly listen and act upon the guidance of the inner voice, and to continually push out of the comfort zone, to grow, risk, and change. It could also mean to be more accepting of those around us and choosing "loving" as a response, and daily allow love to become our strongest emotion. From radio songs, to bumper stickers, little heart decorations everywhere, love is taking on a new prominence. For many years I remember hearing that life *doesn't really change*. No one can say that any longer. It has changed everywhere, whether we like that or not. One of the changes is that we are constantly becoming more aware of other countries and their myriad problems. We are more globally aware with each day passing. If we can shift away from worshipping a god of fear and more towards worshipping a God of Love, all of life will become easier. I wonder who convinced us all that life "is hard"—full of problems. How much more fun to add some laughter; sure, life is full of problems. I'd much rather laugh at them, than cry. And if you can agree with that, then 33/6 is doing its job.

It occurred to me that all the Master Numbers reduce down to even numbers, while 55, 66, 77, 88, and 99 all reduce to unevens. This looks like a numerical *demonstration* of the shift from left hemisphere dominance to right hemisphere dominance —resulting eventually in *balanced* use of our brains.

Someday, somewhere in the future, when all the Master Numbers are in use, they might read like this:

11/2: Spiritual teachers, courageously demonstrating and teaching Earth students to stand each in their own integrity, while being gentle and sensitive with themselves and each other.

22/4: Master builders, constructing a world that bends and gives, uniting everyone into the common cause of peace.

33/6: The grown-up child, playfully inspiring others into greater joy, creativity, and service. Assisting us into more joy and creativity.

44/8: Dedicated workers, establishing a balanced world built on the solid foundation of God's law.

55/1: Adventurers, freely pioneering a new world where each person can freely align themselves with the will of God to experience exciting, creative lives. Money will be a bi-product for work done, not a goal in itself. There will be no fear of being different or wrong, as everyone will be living secure in God's love, being themselves.

66/3: People who teach service as something that comes from a caring heart. Their responsibility will be to demonstrate loving and joy while assisting others to become more aware of the beauty in life.

77/5: Wise ones who can assist others with the experiences necessary to achieve absolute trust and faith in themselves. These people will have specially developed senses so that they can see below the surface and know their own divinity. And from that security live life freely, open to adventure.

88/7: Balancers, bringing evenness into all walks of life, wisely bridging the inner and outer worlds of reality. These will be healing ministries with a deep well of faith and trust.

99/9: Great lovers of life. Teachers and way-showers demonstrating unconditional love and compassion so that all will be able to *feel* it as well as *hear* the words describing it. They will hold in their hearts the knowledge that we are all one.

⋈

CHAPTER THREE

Speaking
The Language

The Inclusion Table

When the witch took away all remembrances of lifetimes past, she stored many traces of them here. This valuable table is a rich source of knowledge of past lifetime accomplishments which can now lead to an understanding of present strengths and weaknesses or imbalances. If we were perfect in all areas, we wouldn't be here, filling in the gaps. This table is a fascinating place to look when comparing two charts as it could be that two people having the same amount of the same numbers, shared those lifetimes, working together. Use this as a key to awaken your intuition.

In reading the table, look *first* for what number is in the highest abundance, then the number that is in the *lowest*. (Keep in mind that shorter names have fewer letters, so *only* compare these numbers with each other, not with "I have more than you do!") Commonly, the numbers 6, 7, and 8 are found in low proportion or are missing altogether.

The highest quantity of numbers in a person's name reveals their greatest strength, while the areas missing often are those of weakness or imbalance. In this instance, *and only at this time*, when looking to see what number is the highest, if there are lots of 5's, *subtract two of them to put the amount of 5's in proper proportion*. (Since the United States was founded on freedom, it might seem natural to find a high proportion of 5's in the names of people living here. And that is the case; in fact, I was interested to see that both U.S.A. and America total to 5, as does July 4, 1776. People living in different countries, with other alphabets, share other traits. Mexico, for instance, is high in 6's and has an extra 9 in their alphabet. Generally, they are much more dramatic, loving, traditional, and family-oriented than North Americans.) So in subtracting two 5's, another number may come forward as the highest. Having no 5's in a name is extremely uncommon in the United States, and if there are only one or two present, this is considered almost none.

People may be completely unaware that they have these strengths, taking them for granted or assuming "everyone's like that." Frequently, these indicate and account for characteristics habitually displayed by a person who is completely unconscious of the fact they are acting out past life patterns. Maybe they are retained as cellular memories or as "ingrained habits."

Here is an important key to unlocking your flow of intuition: remember that bygone times were completely different than today. Push your mind back to what life might have been like long ago and how people working with this number might have behaved as a result of the times. Then, realize anyone wanting to develop even more of the same attribute, is wanting the benefit of our changing times for further development of that strength. For example, it would be a completely different thing to be a strong, courageous woman in the 1600s or at the turn of this century, from what it is today. So if you see someone with lots of the same number in their name and they are still focusing on developing more, ask yourself, "If they have so much of this, why do they want more?" You may be surprised with the answer you get. And, I guess, there never is enough, until perfection is attained.

Many 1's in a name can mean great courage displayed in other lifetimes. It would probably indicate many lives as a man, or if a woman, a strong, self-determined woman who led others or lived by the courage of her own convictions. Of either sex, these could have been the trailblazers of their time. The gift now is great inner strength. The negative side would be someone who is pig-headed and bossy, has little patience with committees or group processes, and finds it difficult to accept help or assistance from anyone.

Many 2's in a name can mean great and unusual ability to work in harmony with others, perhaps from living as a twin or in communal situations with others holding the roles of leadership. It would indicate a high probability of many feminine lives, or as a man, a soft-spoken, gentle person, who flowed with his life rather than exhibited great masculine traits. The gift now is patience and knowledge of the rhythms of life. The negative side could be someone who hates to make up their own mind about anything, always deferring to those around them, is vacillating, insecure and anxious to please.

Many 3's in a name can mean great artistic talents and abilities or a skillful way with words. In other lifetimes, these were the prolific creators of dance, story and song, or clowns and mimes who brought laughter to their times. Their gift now is grace. The negative side could be someone who spends their time gossiping and talking about what they're "going to do someday..." or is prone to temper tantrums, jealousy, or very silent.

Many 4's in a name can mean a hard worker who can display unusual ability to push through all odds to accomplish any goal determined. These are the constructionists of the past; perhaps Freemasons and cathedral builders. They laid the foundations upon which today's societies and cultures are built. Their gift now is dedication. The negative side could be a tendency to limit themselves with such a strong streak of practicality that they fail to see the benefit of anything unless they know its purpose. Or, be prone to being very set in their ways, making things much more difficult than necessary.

Many 5's in a name can mean love of freedom and the untraditional. It is said no boundaries would have been expanded or exploration carried on without the 5's throughout the ages. They have consistently brought change with them as well as freer communication and futuristic, inventive ideas. This could also represent great sensual appetites cultivated in the past. Their gift now is nonconformity, although they might attempt to conceal this. Freedom has never really been a quality easily accepted by others. People being free have been burned, stoned, even exiled for being different, which could remain as a cellular memory called "fear of freedom" — or, "I'll say what I think and get locked up for it." The time for hiding is behind us. Go for it. The negative side could be a great restlessness and instability in their nature with a reluctance to commit to anything, always feeling they need to be free in case something better comes along. This translates to always living for the future, or *someday,* instead of enjoying life right now.

  6's, 7's, and 8's are very common missing numbers, so if there are two or more in a name, that would amount to many.

  Many 6's in a name can mean a strong tendency to martyrdom that sometimes conceals a very loving heart. In other lifetimes, these were the servers, teachers, and nurses who commonly put all others' needs ahead of their own. This indicates a great need for emphasis to be placed on learning to put themself *first.* Their gift now is a great loving heart. The negative side could be someone who takes responsibility for everybody and everything and whose usual response is to feel *guilty* as if whatever went "wrong" was solely their fault, as if no one else had any part in the matter.

  Many 7's in a name is very uncommon. It represents someone who spent many lifetimes looking for God and faith. This may have been in pyramids, ashrams, temples, in ivory towers; yet wherever it was, they were generally alone and have an *unusual* need for aloneness now. They may also not have much experience with the every-dayness of life today, and it may seem very difficult. Their gift now is unique faith in themselves and God. The negative side could be someone who has trouble handling their aloneness and turns to alcohol, drugs, or lives so much inside themselves that they are tortured, melancholy, or depressed.

  Many 8's in a name can mean great and unusual skills with money or special understanding of the law. This may have been someone who had achieved mastery of unusual things, such as powers of the mind, strategy and tactics, perhaps a general or someone involved with court intrigue, stocks, bonds, and investments. Someone skilled as a manipulator. Their gift now is a unique understanding of the laws of karma and the actions of the Light. The negative side could be someone with a violent temper left over from days as royalty or a dictator; a habitual gambler; a tyrannical or compulsive person who constantly criticizes or finds fault with everything.

Many 9's in a name can mean great flair for drama and intensity. It represents someone with unusual caring and depth of feeling as well as unlimited capacity for the appreciation of the beauty of life. This is an old soul who has lived many lifetimes, caring deeply enough to raise the condition of mankind, and working to bring more love and acceptance onto the planet. Their gift now is the thanks and appreciation of many loving hearts who have been touched and transformed by their love. The negative side could be an instability coming from their deep emotional nature so that they experience the widest mood swings and see only the *melodrama* in life. Or, someone who is completely down on everyone and can see no good anywhere.

Missing Numbers are a force in people's lives because they indicate a weakness or undeveloped trait. Frequently, they will show up in the Challenges and Pinnacles as the time *designated* for development. If this is the case, you may expect it to be very challenging, as it's time you selected to "get it now." Whether found in the name, Birthpath, Challenges and Pinnacles, Cycles of Growth, or even on the Planes of Expression (anywhere you can locate it), it represents a desire to strengthen this area. Even if it's not to be found anywhere, this is still a force for improvement. People are usually aware when they are out of balance in an area, expressing too much of a trait or not enough. They welcome knowing this is an undeveloped area, as that frequently explains some of their behavior to them. If you are missing a number and it's not to be found anywhere, you're missing a color and musical note. Find a way to add a dash of it to your life.

If there are no 1's in a name, it can indicate lack of ego and knowledge of self as "I"; easier to think in terms of "we." It also can indicate a much stronger connection with God than most people seem to have. Perhaps the absence of "1" leads to a firmer knowledge of "I." Actually, in all my years of counting the numbers in people's names, I've met only a handful of people missing 1's.

Lesson to be learned: To know themselves and to have the courage to act on their convictions.

Missing 2's in a name can indicate lack of patience, tact, and timing. These people are learning about collecting things. I've read (but have not met anyone who validates this), that these can be kleptomaniacs; somehow it would fit. They are learning to be more delicate, intuitive, and to operate more from a feeling level. Lesson to be learned: about partnerships—how to be more harmonious with the people in your life as well as how to operate within life's rhythms and cycles, with patience.

Missing 3's can indicate little experience with spontaneous creative ability or perhaps a problem with words. These people are learning to freely express the joy of living in all that they say and do. Lesson to be learned: is to lighten up and enjoy life. They frequently feel that they are not creative and don't allow their "child" to play. Try a few things "just for fun;" maybe fingerpainting or something you would never dream of doing. If it makes you laugh at yourself or brings more humor to your life, it's worthwhile.

Missing 4's can indicate little experience with the skills necessary to organize themselves or their lives. Discipline and punctuality could be big issues. Allow others to "show you the ropes" and take advantage of any shortcuts or tips that will offer more knowledge along the lines of practical suggestions for being more efficient.

Something to think about.... It's an interesting concept to think we're frequently programmed by patterns from other lifetimes, inhibited from doing something either because we've never done it before or have done it before with an undesired outcome. I have a sense in this lifetime we're free to push through anything, and it's important that we do. Saying "I'm afraid to try such and such because in another lifetime I..." seems like a strange way to be living in the moment, making each experience new. Fear is something we all have. We can either acknowledge that and continue, or allow it to block us from having an experience that we want. Someday we will live in a world with no fear. I've decided for me I'd like to create that now.

Missing 5's can indicate little experience of the world. Past lives were probably very sheltered or very focused on the job. There may be a tendency to shy away from crowds and be fearful of change or moving around as in past lives there wasn't much opportunity for these things. Take it slowly, allow yourself your fears and work with them. Lesson to be learned: push yourself to be more curious and expansive. Expand your horizons and boundaries.

Missing 6's can indicate little experience with responsibilities (remember this is from the past). Probably there are plenty in this lifetime. This is a very common missing number and it is usual for it to be found in charts of single parents or unmarried couples who say, "What difference does a little piece of paper make?" Lesson to be learned: to take care of *yourself* so that you can take care of others.

Missing 7's can indicate little experience with faith and trust. This is a very common missing number and might easily be the result of many lifetimes of looking for faith and not finding it, living austere lifetimes as a renunciate, nun, or priest, in cold cells doing penance, finding *fear* of faith rather than faith itself. People missing 7's commonly are afraid to trust themselves or anyone else. Lesson to be learned: to trust yourself and believe in the power of love.

Missing 8's can indicate little experience with the money and the business affairs of life. Also, very commonly, fear of authorities. For women, this translates sometimes into fear of men and seeing them as authority figures who will judge, expecting criticism. For men, it's putting other men into father roles and being fearful of standing up to them. Lesson to be learned is around money and power. Learn to handle your material affairs; to balance your checkbook; learn how money grows and the power that is attached to it. *Stand up* to those you cast in authority roles. You may have had others to handle your money affairs in other lives; now it's time for you to get an understanding of this important energy.

Missing 9's (it's unusual to be missing 9's) can mean inexperience in the ways of the world. May indicate someone with little experience of forgiveness and compassion. Lesson to be learned: anything that would teach you more compassion and understanding of the pains and the joys of life. Perhaps it would be helpful to study comparative religion, philosophy, to travel and keep open to what you can learn of life.

ॠ

Planes of Expression

People operate on many different levels. All at the same time, we can be thinking one thing, doing another, experiencing a feeling (such as joy, anxiety, excitement, depression), and have a flash of intuition. "Body language" is very revealing of what a person is saying without the use of words...their physical level is doing the talking. People can communicate telepathically, without opening their mouths. Most of us got conditioned to using the *word* level, the mental, while growing up. "Mommy, why are you angry?" "I'm NOT angry" was enough to confuse any of us. There have been times when I simply couldn't communicate my thoughts to someone or understand what they were trying to say. We weren't on the same "wave length." I would tell myself to listen to the intent, not to the words themselves.

The Planes of Expression focus on the manner in which a person expresses himself in the world physically, mentally, emotionally, and intuitively (or spiritually), or, to make it a little plainer, the way a person thinks, behaves (acts), feels, and senses. While these levels have little to do with what a person *does* in life or who they are, it has lots to do with the manner in which they operate. If a relationship is built on a sound connection in these planes, the people involved can be very different and have completely dissimilar goals yet can read each other's thoughts, be interested in the same things, say the very thing the other person was thinking, have the identical approaches to life; both want to dance all night, both have deep needs for appreciation or get hurt easily in arguments and throw up big walls for defense.

Something to think about.... My observation is that it's easier for most people to connect with their physical and mental levels. We frequently are blocked on the emotional level from all the years of "keeping a stiff upper lip" or demonstrating that we can be "a big girl or boy...." and are not too sure we even *have* an intuitive level as few of us were raised to follow our intuition. "Winging it" is usually not held as a brave, courageous manner in which to attempt to live. Further, as the even numbers represent form and structure, it's easier for them to relate to the tangibles—things that can be seen and touched—than to things with less substance. It appears to be that the uneven numbers can be more emotional and more easily in touch with their intuition. I feel that the Mental and Physical planes represent the left hemisphere of the brain and the Emotional and Intuitive planes are the right brain. In thinking out this process and trying to separate the planes so that they can be helpful, it seems that most forces for movement start either in the mind or the heart, with emphasis in our society in following the head. Yet now we are understanding the need for a balance of both head and heart. Maybe learning to follow more fully the dictates of our hearts, will assist us to come into balance and operate and express from all our planes and levels.

It seems to me that of all the numbers, the aspects represented by the 3 and 5 are the most commonly repressed and inhibited from true expression: 3, as "childishness" that is put aside as we "grow up," and 5 as free expression that is discouraged as we're taught to obey and be conventional. We're taught to sit in neat rows, all stand at once, watch what others are doing, and follow their lead. "Okay, now watch me and do the same as I do" is an instruction we heard frequently in early life. Can you remember: "I told you to wash, do you call *that* clean?" These may have been long ago, yet they certainly shaped and molded us and let the 3's and 5's know their natural desire to do things differently was somehow *not* acceptable. And the left brain dominated with its lists and directions and analytical side in action. Already the message is being transmitted to some babies that it's fine for them to express themselves in their own unique fashion. Someday we'll have joyful, creative 3's and free, adventurous 5's exerting their full influence.

In reading the Planes, look first for which Plane has the highest total. It probably is the manner in which the person handles their problems. They analyze them from the Mental; clean the house or want to punch someone's lights out from the Physical, go for a walk; get Emotional, maybe hysterical; or turn them over to Divine guidance. Please be aware of the seeming contradictions that appear. Bring to mind and remember that each number can easily have a problem with the number next to it in their natural sequence. Allow your own natural sensitivity to operate here. These Planes can be greatly influenced by the other numbers present in the chart.

In a comparison, a sound relationship can be built on compatibility of these levels. It works well if the same number is found as a *total on any Plane*, not especially limited to the same number on the same Plane. Regardless of our careers or destinies in life, if I have a 5 on the Physical and you have too (and if it hasn't been repressed too much and if we've pushed through our fears), we would both want to go adventuring off the beaten track trying things like hang gliding, hot air ballooning, skating, or maybe shooting the white water. However, if I have a 5 physical and you have a 5 Mental with a 2 Physical, you would cringe at the very idea and start telling me of all the "bad things" that could happen, yet — and this is *very* important — would understand why I wanted to go and would be interested to hear all about it when I returned. 6 on the Physical would think I was irresponsible for taking all those chances. If you understand yourself and your general tendencies, it's easier to bravely try something new and lift above the natural hesitancies that are just "your way" and push through your limits to expand yourself into your fullest potential.

In attempting to sum up how each number operates by Planes, I've found some characteristics express from many Planes. Accept that if a number is a total on any Plane, *the characteristics may express through any level*; i.e., if listed as Physical it could also be Mental.

1 on any plane indicates strong feelings and opinions.
Mental: it generally thinks of itself first, takes things very personally, and isn't too accustomed to asking others' advice; has great honor and integrity. Can be very intolerant and impatient with little regard for tradition.
Physical: frequently is a "loner," impatient with teams, committees and group processes — except as boss or team captain. Great executive abilities; displays dignity and individualistic style. Sometimes demonstrates great boldness.

Emotional: whatever 1 does is done in an original manner. It tends to have strong emotions and feelings, yet can conceal them or use them for the effect they will achieve. Capable of great anger that blows over and is gone, and remarkable self-control.

Intuitional: sudden flashes of intuition and inspiration.

2 on any plane is a soft, sensitive number and can be a number of great extremes.

Mental: expresses its thoughts slowly, deliberately, and sometimes not at all. Dislikes arguments, can be very diplomatic preferring peace and tranquility; considerable loyalty and devotion. May feel shy and timid. Frequently suspects it's "stupid," and when in doubt says nothing. It walks away from an argument mumbling, "What I should have told him was...." A good listener; commonly asks others' opinions; thinks in terms of "we;" can be very indecisive and vacillating; likes to save things and have collections.

Physical: can be a very delicate person, not much for competitive sports, much more for dance, declines opportunities to stand out if at all possible. Needs to be near water. Seldom does things alone, is a good actor, can be very adaptable and is generally conservative. May consider itself lazy as it really prefers to "hang out," doing nothing.

Emotional: cries or shows its feelings embarrassingly easy. Some 2's express great balance, others great imbalance. May appear very moody and filled with nameless fears. The 2 needs to take each opportunity to translate its feelings into words. As it does this, it is surprising how much and how deeply it feels and intuits.

Intuitional: the strength of the 2 lies in its intuition. It has so much that it commonly assumes everyone has the same amount or doubts that it has any at all.

3 is the number of the child and can display all the positives and negatives that accompany that. 3 on any plane is a happy, creative number with a good sense of humor.

Mental: Friendly, optimistic with a good imagination, and the ability to see and hear humor in things others miss. It tends to giggle at the most inopportune moments. Joy wells up like a fountain in 3. "Scattered" is especially descriptive when applied to the 3 as it tends to scatter its thoughts, words, energies, possessions, anything. 3 focuses on direct communication through words, and often this is an area that needs the most work. Few of us come into life with well-developed communication skills. 3 needs to find the perfect words for a heartfelt communication and not just fill the air with chatter.

Physical: a bubbly personality, someone who is usually surrounded by clutter, has a hard time disciplining itself to finish things, and loves to be sociable. Playful, versatile and charming, sometimes leaving unfinished projects everywhere. Can have temper tantrums and be involved with love triangles.

Emotional: can be warm, good hearted, easy going with a sunny disposition; also jealous and very demanding.

Intuitional: has the ability to tap the universal mind by simply taking a cat-nap and awakening with a perfect solution. Much of 3's endless creativity comes from this level.

4 on any plane is a planner and doer.

Mental: doesn't like sudden changes, feels most comfortable with established patterns and regimes. Organizes things and is fair, just, loyal, thrifty, and is gifted with a practical approach to life. Loves making lists and reading directions. Can be precise, exacting, and obedient. Conscientiously follows orders and can get bogged down by detail.

Physical: careful of its appearance; probably doesn't like to be dirty, certainly not slovenly. Demonstrates great stamina and inner strength. Is a skillful builder or organizer and works diligently from dawn until dark of night when necessary. Can have a stubborn streak, be serious and quiet.

Emotional: prefers to appear calm and unruffled and can be very uncomfortable when others display sentimentality or other emotions. Tends to keep things bottled up and may not even be in touch with the fact that it has emotions.

Intuitional: may doubt that it has any intuition (not so). If it can recognize intuition at work, it will use it in a very practical manner.

5 on any plane is an attractive, impulsive number that displays endless curiosity.

Mental: a quick wit, a good mind, is open, loves to talk of travel and interesting things, gets bored and impatient easily. 5 has problems with reading and following directions and doing methodical things, it possesses a great sense of humor and lots of enthusiasm. Loves change, new ideas, and has the potential to make instant decisions, yet sometimes finds this difficult as its first choice would be to avoid a decision altogether and have both its cake and eat it. May have difficulties keeping deadlines and tends to be slightly claustrophic and have problems with fears of restriction and commitment.

Physical: boundless energy, loves travel, new places and adventures. Is sexual, sensual, friendly, out-going, versatile and free-spirited. Needs lots of room with few walls, restrictions, or advice from others.

Emotional: is free (if this level has not been completely repressed from childhood) to experience the full range of emotions and express them. This is an aspect of the 5 that can be very difficult for other numbers to comprehend. 5 can run the full gamut of emotions in any given period of time, even the ability to laugh and cry all at once. Has a quick temper and is ruled by the heart; once the flare-up is over, it's gone.

Intuitional: can have great flashes of intuition and almost an instinctual sense of what to do next.

6 on any level is loving, responsible, and has a strong desire to do everything "just right." It's learning to take responsibility for its *own* health and welfare.

Mental: solid, dependable, concerned, patriotic, service-minded and traditional. Thinks of others first and cares about their opinions. 6 is the one you can count on to be strong during an emergency, think of everyone first and fall apart later — even if later never comes. Loves to be in a relationship and can have amazing abilities to adjust or expect everything to be romantically perfect.

Physical: appears cultured, refined, and holds high standards. Responds best to admiration and approval, yet is willing to do most anything to be helpful. May feel guilty when relationships fail, as if there was something more that needed to be done. Loves to share its bed and heart, is home-loving, family-oriented, and *long-suffering*.

Emotional: sympathetic, kind, charming, loyal, generous, giving, and warm, with a tendency to smother. Being a great lover and appreciator of beauty, 6 creates it everywhere. 6's allows itself to feel guilt and resentment and tends to control its other feelings. It's much easier for the 6 to give than to receive. It frequently confuses duty for loving, and is romantic, artistic, helpful, and loves to play mother/nurse. 6 thinks of your needs before you do.
Intuitional: 6 is so outward turned to think of others that it may not think it has any intuition. This level is expressed as concern over the welfare of family, friends, and loved ones.

7 is aloof, observant, reserved on any plane; doing a research paper on "Life on Earth."
Mental: brilliant, independent thinker who analyzes everything. Introspective, impartial, dedicated to honesty. Takes itself and life very seriously; loves to delve into mysteries; treasures knowledge, and can be very secretive, cynical and distrustful. There may be a critical side that tends to find more faults than solutions. Gifted with technical knowledge and a natural affinity with computers and electronics. Sarcastic and witty when hurt.
Physical: needs lots of alone time, prefers quiet and small groups. Is selective with its friends and confidants. Prefers philosophical conversations to sports, and has a problem with disorder, confusion, and noise. Can appear fastidious, reserved, and perfect.
Emotional: appears undemonstrative and doesn't display much emotion, yet can be easily hurt, melancholy, and feel sorry for itself. Is very much the observer in life and loves to probe others' feelings and thoughts. Deep love of beauty and serenity, can be gentle and considerate.
Intuitional: great inner wisdom, mystical nature, flashes of intuition and, at times, amazing insight.

8 on any plane is intelligent, powerful, and strong-willed. 8 symbolizes balance and order (the step before that may look like unbalance and chaos).
Mental: ambitious, loves being an authority, has good judgment and executive ability. Has a strong sense of fairness; can be very moral, upright and honest, or completely on the opposite side of

the law. Things appear very black or white. 8 has great strength of character, self-discipline, and powers of concentration. Can have a harsh, critical side that chatters constantly inside; judging everyone and everything. 8 can be its own worst enemy, expecting everything to be hard. Can display dictator tendencies, firm disciplinarian, commands respect.

Physical: enormous drive, great stamina and inner strength. Possesses an active, dominant personality with great loyalty to the few it respects. Can be very competitive and involved with rebellion or revolt. Is comfortable with a great display of wealth and affluence and can have the Midas touch. Seldom satisfied with mediocrity, it's the work-a-holic. Does things in extremes. Can be involved in "near-death" experiences or live many lives in this lifetime.

Emotional: great passion for causes and concerns close to its heart. Can appear indifferent, is fair minded and just. Can be jealous, possessive, display great bursts of anger and discomfort with anyone's tears. Can have a well-hidden streak of sentimentality.

Intuition: fine intuition in regard to business and commerce. Keen powers of perception, abilities to weigh, balance, and estimate strengths and weaknesses.

9 on any level is highly idealistic and capable of touching the heart of the universe. Some 9's have an unusually deep connection with the "world" (a word that vibrates to 9) and are able to predict earthquakes or natural disasters by some inner feeling.

Mental: philanthropic, concerned, and service-minded. 9 is broad and impersonal in its outlook with a great flare for the melodramatic which colors all it thinks or does; a sincere desire to better conditions for everyone. 9 has a deep need for the love and appreciation it so easily gives to others.

Physical: loves to surround itself with beauty, rarely displays jealousy or possessiveness. Can be impractical with money and possessions, and yet whatever is given away comes back in one form or another. Possesses great strength and ability to act out life. Wants to *rescue* everyone.

Emotional: ardent nature, feelings capable of soaring from the heights of rapture to the depths of despair all in one afternoon.

Understanding in outlook, yet easily wounded by the depth of its love. Can be sympathetic, warm-hearted, sensitive, compassionate, and also impersonal and distant.

Intuitional: deep insightful nature, gifted with psychic abilities, perceptive, great innate intelligence, special healing gifts.

0 It is possible to have no numbers on any of the Planes. This would give the freedom to respond at any given time in ANY manner. To have any of the above numbers on any Plane, channels the behavior along the lines of that digit. *0* on any plane represents freedom of expression — unlimitedness.

Name Changes

Deciding to change your name, whether through marriage or in any manner, announces that you have concluded what was to be done with the first one and are moving on. Get your goal real clear. Do you want a name to add beauty, strength, fame, fortune, confidence? Generally this may be a step in the right direction. Many famous people have benefited from it. Long ago in India, a letter was added to a name to bring increased health.

Now approach this slowly so you'll get the best results. Perhaps you have an intuitive hint of the new name from a dream or in meditation; if not, suggest to your subconscious that you want the perfect one to appear. It may jump out at you from an unexpected source such as a street sign, the book you're reading, or come in a dream.

- Gather together a list of the names you favor.
- Put them into the order of choice.
- Then do the numbers on all of them.

It's highly desirable for your name and birthday to total to the same. Yet, if your desire is for more fun and joy in your life, having them both total "7's" wouldn't get that result. So don't make that be a hard-and-fast rule. My experience is that when they're put into order by choice, the first choice is usually the best. Do a full chart including the Planes of Expression and Inclusion and lay out who is this person that you are wanting to become and see how it feels. This is also very helpful for choosing business names. Use the incorporation date or day of opening as the Birthday. For businesses, pay special attention to the Missing Number and Birthpath. A "1" Personal Year is an especially favored time to start using your new name. There are books in the library with instructions on how to change your name legally without paying attorney's fees.

There are even choices to be made in marrying and remarrying. Play with the name, adding middle names or hyphenating the last names, until it feels just right to you — it's too important to leave to "chance." When two people have a special energy connection and one changes their name, that *can* be the beginning of the end. In a marriage, my first choice would be for both to hyphenate *both* names to share the full experience. Otherwise, by changing her name the wife is adding another "game board" on top of her own while the husband is allowing that, yet making no changes at all.

Now, if what you're using is *not* on the birth certificate, treat it as a name change. I can still perceive the influence of my name at birth even though I have used Ruth Drayer far longer than my maiden name.

7 Heart's Desire and Personality with a 5 Destiny certainly are the numbers of someone who could grow up and do something as untraditional as professional Numerologist. Even my original Planes of Expression are accurate. However, while someone with those numbers might certainly write a Numerology book, it wouldn't be one about having *fun* in life and *loving* the world. That can be attributed to my 9 Heart, 3 Destiny and Personality. I am the combination of both sets of numbers, one set *overlaid* on top of the other. In answer to the question, "Which am I," I'm *both*. In Numerology, we seldom subtract...we just keep adding. For people who've had many names in their lives, use only the current name. So, to get an accurate picture, work out the full name at birth and the present signature. And by that, I mean the name you think of yourself as...or the name you would offer me if we were being introduced. That's a bit complicated, and we certainly all are.

MORE ON BIRTHDAYS

The birthday we select is of utmost importance as it symbolizes our major lesson. My mother once told me her labor started ten days before I arrived, then quit. She asked why I'd changed my mind. It made me think how different my life could have been. With the same name, I'd have the same character traits, personality, etc., yet many of my life experiences would have varied completely, and maybe been less interesting.

The month, day, and year of birth, structure an intricate pattern of interacting cycles with the Birthpath as the main theme. Throughout life, it's always there, being developing more fully.

The Cycles of Growth divide the Birthpath into three sections. Each section influences for approximately 28 years. What's being developed in each of these sections is symbolized by the *reduced digit of the birth month, the birth day, and the birth year. The birth month influences from birth to 28 years*; is called the CYCLE OF YOUTH. *The birth day* influences from *28 years until 56*; is called the CYCLE OF MATURITY. *The birth year* influences from *56 to whenever*; is called the CYCLE OF WISDOM. Amelia's cycles: Cycle of Youth = 7, Cycle of Maturity = 6, Cycle of Wisdom = 8. To find them, reduce your birthday into three single digits.

Amelia's birthday was July 24, 1898 = 7 + 6 + 8 = 21 = 3.

Her Cycle of Youth = 7 (her month)
Cycle of Maturity = 6 (her day)
Cycle of Wisdom = 8 (her year)
What are yours?

AN ADVANCED LOOK AT THE PINNACLES AND CHALLENGES

The method of working with the Pinnacles and Challenges completely reduced is helpful for the beginner. More and deeper insight can be obtained by using the birthday numbers in the original *unreduced* form and *reducing* the *birth year* to only *two digits.*

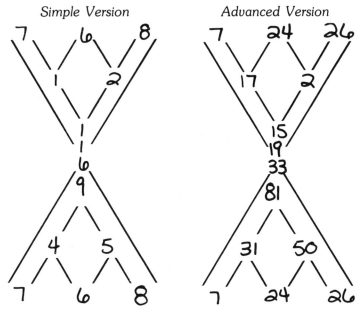

Simple Version	*Advanced Version*

Greater insight can be obtained by seeing deeper. For instance, if an 8 can be reduced from 17, 26, 35, 44, 53, etc., each 8 will be different. Interpret each of these number's compounds as *single digits that are working together.* Frequently, this longer method brings to light additional Challenges. They *all* are operating in the designated time period. The more understanding you can have into a period, the easier it is to accept gracefully.

Actually, wherever there's a day, month, and year it's possible to do the Pinnacles and Challenges even dividing an entire day into four cycles: 2:00-8:00 A.M., 8:00-2:00 P.M., 2:00-8:00 P.M., and 8:00-2:00 A.M. If you want deeper insight into a special day in your life, do the Challenges and Pinnacles. Try using your *own* Personal Day, Month, and Year (see following page), as well as the Calendar Day, Month, and Year, to see which feels more accurate to you.

Personal Cycles

In Numerology, 9 is the length of all cycles. We each have a PERSONAL YEAR cycle, found by adding together our *month of birth, our day,* and the *present calendar* year. Amelia's Personal Year in 1990 would have been 5:

$$\begin{array}{lcl} \text{Birth Month} = & 7 \\ \text{Birth Day} \quad = & 6 \\ 1990 \quad\quad\quad = & \underline{1} \\ & 14 = 5 \end{array}$$

We each have a PERSONAL MONTH cycle, found by adding together our PERSONAL YEAR plus the *PRESENT CALENDAR month.*

We each have a PERSONAL DAY cycle, found by adding our PERSONAL YEAR plus our PERSONAL MONTH plus the PRESENT CALENDAR DAY.

And finally, a special magical day occurs three *times each month* called the SPIRITUAL BIRTHDAY. To find yours: every time the month and day *combined equal the number of your own birthday* (reduced down), it is a day of power for you and a time to do something wonderful for yourself—remember, three times every month!

Everything you've learned from Personal Years apply to the Personal Months and Personal Days. The only difference being that with shorter durations, their impact is not quite as great. I've observed that personal months overlap about one week into each month. Perhaps it takes a while for the influence to wane from the previous month. In my own personal life, I find personal years and months very helpful, and personal days a little restrictive. I scarcely notice them. I guess I want to make each day what I want it to be. I pay more attention the Universal or Calendar Day, which is found by adding the *day* plus the *month* plus the *year* (or today's date) and reducing it.

Personal Years

Within the framework established by the Challenges and Pinnacles there is a nine-year Personal Cycle. The Personal Years grow organically, one out of the other, unfolding as gently as a flower garden—starting from 1, as with the idea to have a garden; 2 prepares the ground; 3 plants; 4 waters/thins/weeds; 5 watches everything sprout; 6 admires the garden, harvests; 7 analyzes the yield; 8 markets; 9 turns the land under for the next garden, loving the goodness, and *appreciating* the bounty of nature. For me, this is one of the most beautiful parts of Numerology, because it is here that I can perceive the pattern and flow of each life. This is where to look to do realistic goal-setting and life-planning—going with the flow instead of fighting it.

When does the Personal Year start? The answer is one of the "controversial" issues of Numerology. I believe it starts January 1 at 12:01 a.m. As the world enters a new vibration, we all enter a new Personal Year. It's easier to perceive for people with birthdays January to June, than June to December. There are two cycles: an Inner that goes birthday-to-birthday, and Outer that goes by the calendar year; some people spend much of each year in 2 cycles.

Now that you are this far into the cycles, you have accomplished a lot. Pat yourself gently and know this will get easier every time you do it. And although it seems complicated at first, it will be second nature to you before long. It is an important portion of the information Numerology has to offer.

Only with a "1" Birthpath does the first nine year cycle begin with the first year of life. With the Birthpath Number, we have also discovered the *number* of the *year* of the cycle in which you were born.

What is your Birthpath number? And, therefore, what year of the nine-year cycle were you born into?

A 1 Personal Year is a year of high energy for beginning things, and is especially welcome after completing the previous cycle. In its enthusiasm, it can run in many different directions, starting new things everywhere. Approach the new year with caution; many new doors will be opening to you at this time, and there is no way in which they can all be entered at once. Save yourself a few steps; allow things to unfold gently instead of rushing into them. If something is meant as your clear new beginning, it will wait. Otherwise, it will disappear into thin air. Don't push too hard. Some of the doors may open from the inside out! Actually, it is *September* before you are in the 1 *Personal Month* of your 1 *Personal Year* (see personal month explanation), so while you are in an opening phase of your life, start to use new eyes with which to appreciate each situation, person, place and thing. Approach it all, no matter what, as if it were the first time you had ever seen it. You are a new person this year, and don't drag along any unnecessary baggage—this applies to any level: old opinions, fears, decisions, choices, judgments, as well as more physical things. Be ready to greet it all with freshly opened eyes—create it new! Get real clear on what you want, then go for it. This is your year for *courage.* What does that mean in your life?

The 2 Personal Year: This number is always a little difficult to talk about, because it represents feelings more than words. After the high energy of a 1 year, 2 comes in with much more softness. It's teaching patience, tact, diplomacy, and sensitivity. Associated with the Moon, it can be very receptive, even appear indecisive or vacillating, because where the 1 asked you to get clear on what you want, the 2 asks that you surrender that for the highest good. With heightened sensitivity, you can look for many things to occur, including greater "extrasensory experiences," more fears, maybe even more tears. It's all fine, and part of the year. 2 is attempting to make you supple, fluid, and flexible. That might feel like the smelting process feels to copper or gold. Just be very patient and do things that will keep you in balance—walk a lot, and swing your arms as you do. Music is very important right now. Dance, or just enjoy listening or playing; read and utilize any information on balancing the hemispheres of the brain. Wash frequently, and sip water constantly. Realize you are in a particularly sensitive time of your life and might have a tendency to blow things all out of proportion. 2 loves to look for tiny little details, collect them, and hold on to them forever. Fight this tendency by telling yourself it may not even be the way it appears to you. This personal year is about partnerships, all and any kind, and finding harmony through tactfulness (not avoidance, but tact). If this year is about partnerships, there is a strong probability that will be your area of harmony—or inharmony. If there are partnership problems, you would be having the same problems with whomever you were with—it's not *their* personal year, it's yours. Focus on what you can learn about being a better partner and communicating with more clarity. 2 has a great tendency to avoid confrontation, so I'm emphasizing this strongly. Learning to openly communicate, with love, is a big step in our education these days. Be gentle and patient with yourself as you learn. Drawing on the experiences of this year, you will soon be sharing these sensitive communication skills with others, assisting in creating greater harmony. This is your year for *cooperation*. What does that mean in your life?

If the 2 Year Adds to 11: all above applies. In addition, there could be an emotional aspect or great indecision and confusion. You need lots of gentle patience with yourself. Also, the year could have a strong emphasis on spirituality with you being a leader to others, even while you feel indecisive and unsure of yourself. (It's amazing how others persist in seeing us in a different light than we see ourselves; how thankful I am for it!) Rest and don't push yourself too hard.

The 3 Personal Year: Look around at the abundance with which this earth has been created. All the different leaves, grasses, trees, flowers, clouds, rocks, people, fertile imaginations, minds, stars in the sky; as you look, realize you are looking at what unlimited creativity through endless joy of expression looks like. This is your year to try it out, to get the feel of unlimited joy through creativity. Express yourself through every medium you can imagine and then push yourself to imagine more. This is your year to play at things, not master them; to be innocent, childlike, joyful, and exuberant. Let your words be positive and loving, and inspire yourself and others to move closer to living in a world of no fear. Stay in the moment and find the joy of spirit within you. Speak the words of a child living in *this* moment—there are no yesterdays, only tomorrows. While this may be joy for some, it may be real work for others. This is your year to plant without concern for what will come up—optimistic planting! Next year, in the 4, you can worry about thinning and transplanting. An analogy that I love for the 3 year is that it's the space in time between caterpillar and butterfly. While it may look like you're running around in circles doing nothing, in reality you're spinning a cocoon. It's the 5 year before you actually see what's coming up where. Some people are actually re-creating themselves at this time, which can be very difficult. However it manifests, and within which Challenge and Pinnacle it occurs, enjoy it, find the humor, and lighten up. The big cosmic joke is that we take it all so seriously. This is your year to be *lucky*. What does that mean in your life?

The 4 Personal Year is the worker. This is your time for weeding, hoeing, transplanting, fertilizing; generally laying down good solid foundations on which the remainder of your cycle will stand. Discipline yourself and lay a thorough foundation so that what you build on top will be sitting solidly. Learn all you can about promptness, efficiency, organization; put your ideas down in writing. The 3 year was for unlimited ideas, this year is for giving them some form. If you knew that this year was a time in which to prepare for the freedom of next year, what steps would you take? What groundwork would you lay? That might mean taking some classes, workshops, or expanding yourself to accumulate knowledge of things which interest you. Begin to prepare yourself for the unexpected opportunities that often come in a 5 Personal Year so that you'll be ready for them; *this is one of the advantages of knowing Numerology*. Now is the time to practically plan for the future. We hear so much about goal planning. Realize you've been doing this easily and well for years—it's as simple as planning to brush your teeth and doing it, or planning to make dinner, serving and eating it. Acknowledge to yourself your proficiency in these things and expand it to learn more practicality in *every* phase of your life. This is your year for *discipline*. What does that mean in your life?

If the 4 Year Adds to 22: all above applies. In addition, there will be *limitless* opportunities for you to bring other things together. Focus on the fact that deep down, everyone wants "it" to work and are waiting to be shown the way. Develop your skills for tuning in and assisting others as arbitrator. Discipline yourself to hold onto the dream of a world in harmony. There can be no vision without someone to hold it. Many of your lessons may come with trying to please too many others and not taking *you* into account. Remember, you are the one with the vision; don't give in for the sake of peace.

The 5 Personal Year is a special time to risk, adventure, and push yourself into new areas of challenge and growth. You are *expanding* yourself *into* your *most unlimited you*. This is an important time to realize that your fears often block you from living the fullness of life; ask yourself: "Why do I allow that?" Whose life is this you are living this time around, anyway? Is there a *good reason* for not doing something you were told not to? Expand yourself through your limits—there are NONE, really, except those you set. This is your year to realize you are an unlimited being. Go hot air ballooning, deep sea diving, hang gliding, read on subjects of which you know nothing. This year focuses a lot on travel—to the inner worlds as well as the outer realms. Eat, smell, touch something new, listen for new sounds—expand all your senses! wkzrsuvi! Play games with yourself to make sure you do at least one new thing every day, no matter how small. Change can be very subtle, as subtle as seeing this word, "wkzrsuvi," now for the second time, and recognizing it as something you have seen before. When the 5 year occurs during a 5 Challenge or Pinnacle, you may be a completely different person before the year is over—certainly a lot freer and more flexible. Learn to roll with the changes and love them—they are the spices of life. This is your year to *adventure*. What does that mean in your life?

The 6 Personal Year says "Okay, let's settle down now and bring that air of freedom and expansion into more established areas; to serve the family, home, and community with more love and devotion." This is an important year for you to learn true service and dedication to yourself. Learn that if you take good care of yourself, everyone benefits; if you run around trying to please everyone, chances are you please no one and may get incredibly frustrated and resentful. 6 has a tendency toward resentments, so be careful what you agree to. Joyful giving and service are very different than doing things you feel you must. Learn how to appreciate yourself. Notice all that you always do for others. Learn to thank *yourself* so that you're not dependent on others for that. If you choose to do something, you then have put yourself in the role of creator, not victim. Take care of your physical body and nurture yourself with beauty. 6 represents marriage and divorce, so that can easily be a significant part of this year if applicable. Everyone benefits if you learn to be your own best friend. This year is about loving. You might ask yourself the question, "What does loving look like, feel like, sound like, etc." In my opinion, it has nothing to do with how much I *"do"* for someone, it's more the feeling I carry inside than what I *do*. Sometimes love looks like standing back and doing nothing except whispering to yourself, "God bless you, I love you" or being a firm disciplinarian. This is your year for *devotion to you*. What does that mean in your life?

The 7 Personal Year: is one of the clearest ways in which to perceive that life is change. That a 6 (which is so tuned in to helping and serving) can turn into a 7 always fascinates me. The 7 virtually says, "Okay, I've served enough." The 7 is the sabbatical year and takes the year off from life, to go inside itself, to look for real meaning and faith. This can be a difficult year on relationships and marriages, and has *nothing to do* with the other person in the relationship. No matter who you're with, you may be feeling more detached and into yourself. 7 can feel isolated from life in varying degrees this year, depending upon how much 7 energy is present from other places in the chart. When I go into a 7 year, I sometimes feel invisible, almost as if no one can hear me. 7 is the observer of life, trying to analyze, collect the data and statistics, and make some sense out of things. Take some time to be alone every day. If that makes things difficult on others, realize you are doing it for them as well as for yourself. Everyone benefits when you have peace of mind, and that is what you are seeking this year. You are looking for answers to questions that can only be answered by turning within, and quiet time is definitely required for that. Whether you space out, daydream, meditate, watch the clouds go by; whatever you do, take time for you. Ask your questions inside. You may feel as if you don't know anything, and in reality you know everything. Waking up tired in the mornings can indicate that you are doing big work in your dream time. As 7 is a special number, this is a very unique year. Find a way to incorporate more ceremony and celebration. Greater wisdom may be your blessing. You are becoming a bridge, making a stronger commitment to serve as a light worker. God and all the angels are with you always, and especially at this time, no matter how alone you may feel. This is your year to achieve *inner peace*. What does that mean in your life?

8 Personal Year is back into the material world to deal with the law and powerful people. Watch what gives them their power. Stand up for what seems fair and just to you. Assert yourself. There may be many confrontations. Take each one as an opportunity to move more into your own personal power. The goal of this year is to balance the material with the spiritual. It is a year of paying back karma and learning to take full responsibility for your thoughts and actions. If you think you're right, you generally are. Allow others to realize this and take more direction and control of things. Keep the word *balance* uppermost in your mind. What does that mean in your life?

9 Personal Year is a time for completions. A good year to to throw away old memories, clothes, ideas, clean out all the closets *on every level*. If you feel inclined to make a will, act on that. If you need to grieve, go ahead. Do whatever needs to be done to finish a complete nine-year cycle so that you can go on fresh next year. If an old lover comes back, ask yourself if this is a completion or a new beginning. If it's the latter, it will come back next year in a new form. Don't try to hold on to anything. That doesn't mean it's all gone — only that it needs to change its form into something better

Most of all, this year is about *forgiveness*. Give yourself a TREAT and let go of *all the stuff* you are still holding against yourself. If you knew then what you know now, it would have been completely different. This year is about love. Treasure it as very special. This is your year of *forgiveness*. What does that mean in your life?

☙

༰

The Table

of Events

Constructing the Gameboard

Goal: To construct the TABLE OF EVENTS and diagram the full timetable in which all the influences for a single year or a span of years can be read at a glance.

We are going to put everything together and plot out each year so that we can see the impact the name and the birthday have on our life. It is an interesting way to observe the life patterns and tune into the similarities that sometimes reoccur, or appreciate a period that was a specially unique, once-in-a-lifetime event.

Amazing as this sounds, the letters of a name (combined with the numbers) represent the tests and opportunities inherent in that life; the value of each number symbolizes the amount of years its influence will be felt. You might observe that a change occurs when one letter ends, and another begins.

Line 1. Plot out the years of your life. Start with the birth year and continue on as long as you want to take it.

Line 2. Fill in your age, *leaving a blank space under the birth year* as it is a full year before we turn one.

Lines 3, 4, and 5. Fill in the letters of the name, *repeating each letter for the amount of the value it holds*: A, J and S influence for one year; B, K and T influence for two years; C, L and U influence for three years; etc. The first name belongs on the first line; whatever the name's total value, that is the amount of years it will take to go through it once. Example: Amelia totals 23, so it would take 23 years to complete the first cycle of the first name. When completed, repeat it until the present or as far into the future as you care to go. Take as many lines as you need with *one full line* for each name.

Line 6. THE ESSENCE is the *total of the values of the letters added vertically*, and represents the overtone of that year.

Line 7. Fill in the Personal Year, *place your Birthpath number directly under the birth year*. This establishes which year of the cycle you were born into. It also identifies where that year fell within the Pinnacle and Challenge

Line 8. Enter the timing of the Pinnacles and Challenges. Be attentive that these *always end in a nine Personal Year;* if they don't, go back and find your error.

Line 9. A full lifetime timetable has been constructed. All the influences for any single year or span of years can be seen at a glance. With practice, this can become incredibly insightful. I find it of great value in understanding and making peace with the past. It's possible to construct charts for your parents and actually see the environment and the problems they were facing at the time of your

TABLE OF EVENTS

AGE		1	2	3	4	5	6	7	8	9	10	11	12	13	14	15	16	17	18	19	20	21	22	23
	1898	99	00	01	02	03	04	05	06	07	08	09	10	11	12	13	14	15	16	17	18	19	20	21
		A	M	M	M	M	E	E	E	E	E	L	L	L	I	I	I	I	I	I	I	I	I	A
		M	M	M	M	A	R	R	R	R	R	R	R	R	Y	Y	Y	Y	Y	Y	Y	M	M
		E	E	E	E	E	A	R	R	R	R	R	R	R	R	H	H	H	H	H	H	H	H
ESSENCE		10	13	13	13	10	15	23	23	23	23	21	21	21	27	25	24	24	24	24	24	24	21	13
PER YEAR	3	4	5	6	7	8	9	1	2	3	4	5	6	7	8	9	1	2	3	4	5	6	7	8
CHALLENGE	1 ←																							
PINNACLE	4 ←																							

birth. As to the future, remember—*nothing* has to be what it was—there is always *free will* to make things different. Once a divorced woman told me about her "wonderful" astrologer who had predicted she would be divorced within two years, and she was. Now if the woman wanted to get out of her marriage, that was one thing; but if, when problems arose, she said, "Well, the astrologer said I was getting divorced and here it is," that's another. Especially common times for divorce would be under the influence of 6, representing "marriage and divorce;" under a 2, "partnerships;" a 5, "freedom;" or a 9, "completions." Yet, it also would work that you would be aware that a difficult time was present. You could choose to get counseling and work through that period together and salvage something very valuable. I find if I'm aware in some way of what's coming, then I will have more choices available to me. Also, I notice how differently I handle things now compared to the first few times those lessons appeared. Experience is not just the best teacher, it's the only teacher.

Although some books include sections on the meanings of the essence, I have found it works better for me to simply read the letters and essences, year by year, and continue to remember the numbers *are the same* wherever I encounter them. In this manner, I call up more intuition to comprehend the developments. In doing sessions with others, I commonly explain the influences and ask them what was happening, and am fascinated by their choices. The more you'll practice with this, the more meaningful it will become.

24	25	26	27	28	29	30	31	32	33	34	35	36	37	38	39	40	41	42	43	44	45	46	47	48	49	50
22	23	24	25	26	27	28	29	30	31	32	33	34	35	36	37											
A	M	M	M	M	E	E	E	E	E	L	L	L	\	\	\											
M	M	A	R	R	R	R	R	R	R	R	Y	Y	Y	4												
A	R	R	R	R	R	R	R	R	T	T	E	E	E	E												
6	17	14	22	22	23	23	23	23	23	14	14	15	21	21	21											
9	1	2	3	4	5	6	7	8	9	1	2	3	4	5	6											
							→	1	2	←																
							→	4	5	←																

Universal Cycles

Just as individuals have personal cycles, so too does the world. Wherever there is a date, it can be translated into cycles. Whether you are interested in going back in time, or into the future, dates can be added to reveal a deeper significance for that day.

•The *Universal Year* is found by simply reducing the year value to a single digit.

•The calendar month plus the year = the *Universal Month.*

•The day, month, and year are all totaled and reduced for the *Universal Day.* Example:

> February 4, 1988 = 2 + 4 + 8 = 5 Universal Day;
> February (2) + 1988 (8) = 1 Universal Month;
> 1988 = 8 Universal Year.

It's very interesting to look back through time at the decades and epochs from the standpoint of their numerical values. Since 1 represents courage to be individual, starting with the year 1000, every year prefaced by 1 has indicated a goal of developing self-reliance and inner strength. 1 is the pioneer, and these times have certainly been periods of massive explorations into every conceivable field. We have blazed trails everywhere, inside our planet

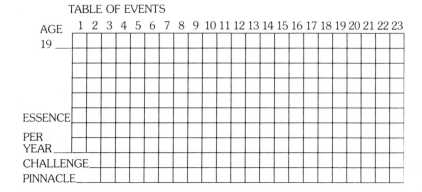

TABLE OF EVENTS

and ourselves, as well. We have also pioneered as far as possible out into space.

A Numerological overview of our recent history: The goal of the '50s was more freedom; the goal of the '60s was to take that freedom and break up the traditional ways of living; i.e., the riots in colleges across the country, the marches and pushes for greater equality across color and sex lines. The goal of the '70s was to bring more spirituality into our lives; people were asking "Is God dead?" and Westerners started meditating, reading Edgar Cayce books, and digging for inner peace. The goal of the '80s was balance between the material and the spiritual worlds. It was a time of integrating the achievements of the '70s into the worlds of money and power. The '80s will be remembered for overthrowing governments and learning to discern right from wrong, good from bad. Because of it, the balance of our world may have shifted into greater equality and stability with God as a living force in our lives (which was what Pythagoras desired to prove those long years ago). The '90s have the potential of being a time of great forgiveness, allowing us the acceptance and compassion necessary to bring about a more global consciousness. It may assist us to see each other as loving flesh-and-blood individuals more than labels or statistics. From this point, we'll be able to move toward achieving what the 2000s symbolize: partnership and harmony. We will have run the "1" out to its logical conclusion—that the time has come to put 1 and 1 together and create the kinship necessary to preserve life on Planet Earth.

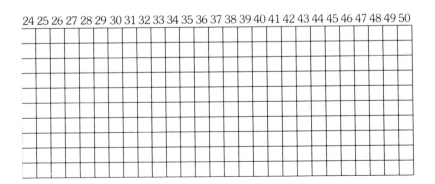

24 25 26 27 28 29 30 31 32 33 34 35 36 37 38 39 40 41 42 43 44 45 46 47 48 49 50

AMELIA
4 3
7

MARY
4 9
4

EARHART
98 92

PUTNAM
7 25 4
9

BIRTH DATE JULY 24 1898
SIMPLIFIED

⃝ = BIRTHPATH

AGES:
0 - 33
33 - 42
42 - 51
51 —

ADVANCED

ATTAINMENT: 1

CHALLENGES

PINNACLES

HEART'S DESIRE ④ ⑦ ⑨
DESTINY 3 8
PERSONALITY 8

PLANES OF EXPRESSION:
MENTAL: 6 EMOTION: 2
PHYSICAL: 4 INTUITION: 5

INCLUSION TABLE
1. 5
2. –
3. 1
4. 2
5. 2
6. 1
7. –
8. 1
9. 4
    17

TABLE OF EVENTS

AGE	1	2	3	4	5	6	7	8	9	10	11	12	13	14	15	16	17	18	19	20	21	22	23	24	25	26	27	28	29	30	31	32	33	34	35	36	37
	A	M	M	M	A	R	R	R	R	R	R	R	R	R	R	R	R	H	H	H	H	M	M	M	A	R	R	R	R	R	R	R	R	T	T	E	E
	E	E	E	E	E	E	E	E	E	L	L	L	L	L	R	Y	Y	Y	Y	Y	M	M	M	M	M	E	E	E	E	E	L	L	L	L	L	L	E

ESSENCE	10	13	13			10	15				23	21	21	21	21		27	25	24	24	24	24	24	13	6	17	14	22	22	22	23	23	23	14	14	15	21	21	21
PER YEAR 3	4	5	6	7	8	9	1	2	3	4	5	6	7	8	9	1	2	3	4	5	6	7	8	9	1	2	3	4	5	6	7	8	9	1	2	3	4	5	6
CHALLENGE 1																																			2			
PINNACLE 4																																			5			

How to Read a Chart

*T*here is no hard-and-fast rule on the "proper way" to read a chart. Over the years, it has changed for me many times—that chart is there to share its secrets with you, and, as I mentioned earlier, those secrets will deepen as you understand more and are more comfortable to say things as you perceive them. If a circle of people were standing around a striped, multi-colored beach ball, and each one said the color they saw, who would be correct? (Answer: Everyone.) So that is how we perceive life. Start reading the chart with whatever piece of information interests you the most.

In reading the chart, I usually look first at the Inclusion Table to see a person's strengths and weaknesses. Next, I look at the rest of the name to see the manner in which they are using these things. It's fairly common to find a missing number showing up on a Plane of Expression. For instance, a person may be missing 2's and have a 2 on the mental plane. This would indicate the person was actively setting out to learn tact and patience through the "school of hard knocks." In my name, I have only two 5's which, please recall, is the number from which to *subtract* two to put it into proportion with the other numbers. Therefore, two 5's is a very small amount. I have a 5 on the mental plane, a 5 Destiny number, and even my Birthpath is a 5. So, starting with the Inclusion Table offers a little insight into a person's weak areas that are now being fortified. Also, it offers you, the reader, a little broader appreciation of this soul you are reading for...as "Wow, they've done this and this, now they're tackling this part; no wonder they have trouble with that area."

1. I generally begin with the Birthpath, feeling that no matter what name we're using, birthday information stays the same.

2. Then I read the Pinnacles and Challenges, scanning the past, spending lots of time on the present (especially noticing the

compatibility of present influencing numbers), and I glance at the future.

3. At the same time, I take the Inclusion Table into account to see which numbers are being strengthened. One of their missing numbers would clearly add to the intensity of the period.

4. Then I go on to the name...how compatible are their numbers, inside themselves and compared to the Birthpath. If each number tends to have a problem with the one next to it, you will be able to immediately spot an area of inner conflict. Before sitting down with someone, try to guess which of these numbers predominates so you can get more familiar with the energies. Having "guessed," be open to listen and learn from them. Each person is so unique, don't presume to tell them *how* they handle their life. They'll tell you once you can explain the energies.

5. Look again at the Inclusion Table to see how it fits with the name.

6. Then, on to the Planes of Expression. (It's common to find a missing number appearing on one of the planes.)

7. The Attainment. (The amount of time I spend with this depends on the age of the person I'm reading — obviously older people would derive more benefit than younger ones.)

8. Next, the Table of Events. Look at each letter and savor the full flavor of each name — strengths and weaknesses. I read the Essence and look if they have experienced the same essence before; maybe they can see a resemblance between those periods of their life. I look at the letters influencing them — and look at what went before, and what comes next.

9. Finally, the Personal Year and the Personal Month, with a discussion of what comes next...and how that fits into the Pinnacle and Challenge.

Everything in the chart is in *relationship* to everything else. Each little piece of information is valuable. Please stay positive as you read the chart—it's only life, and we're all doing it the best way we know. Time and experience will be the best teacher here. This is the part no book can give you, and it comes with an understanding of the number, with a *feel of the energy* it represents, and *lots of practice.* Once you have the feel, next try and sense how it would feel placed next to or in interaction with another. My grandmother had many expressions that she used that were straight from Numerology. She would say, "I've got your number," or, in speaking of my Grandpa, "He only thinks of Number One." She'd comment someone was at "6's and 7's," and I frequently think of her and send her a little blessing when I come across that pattern: 6 thinks its job here is to be responsible and serve; it has a strong tendency to feel guilty when it's not doing either of those things. 7, on the other hand, needs a lot of alone time, off by itself somewhere. So, with a 6 and 7 both present, when the 7 is off by itself the 6 feels guilty for taking time when someone probably needs them; and when 6 is in the middle of being responsible, the 7 feels resentful that it can't be alone. Just explaining this pattern can be a help.

People frequently ask what would be good numbers to seek in a relationship. I don't know that I've ever known anyone who set out to have a relationship with someone by checking their numbers first. That's like going to buy a painting by taking an empty frame. If you've ever tried this, you know it's pretty impossible. Anyway, most people, myself included, have to be attracted to someone before they even care what their numbers are. However, this is a key point to remember: you may discern compatibility and many other things, but I doubt there's a method to accurately calculate the degree of "chemistry" that will be in a relationship nor the amount of love between two people. I've seen and been in relationships that were "made in heaven" according to the numbers, and they went nowhere, and I was very relieved when they did. Years ago, briefly, I was a partner in a computerized dating service using Numerology. We saw some amazing things take place between people who "should" have been "perfect" for each other. This is a good example of free will…and karma, as well. So I want to explode the myth that there is a "perfect" relationship. Generally, people who are friends, or are drawn to each other, have numbers in common.

7/5	GEORGE	97	③	1	6/5	PALMER	7 34 9 /5
(1/2)	3	4	1	PUTNAM	7 25 4 /9		22/4

BIRTH DATE SEPT. 7 1887

SIMPLIFIED

ADVANCED

6 = ④ BIRTHPATH

AGES:
0-32
32-41
41-50
50 —

CHALLENGES   PINNACLES

ATTAINMENT: 4

INCLUSION
TABLE
1. 2
2. 1
3. 2
4. 2
5. 4
6. 4
7. 4
8. 1
9. 2
   /18

HEART'S DESIRE 8
DESTINY 9
PERSONALITY 1

PLANES OF EXPRESSION:
MENTAL: 2   EMOTION: 4
PHYSICAL: 6 INTUITION: 6

TABLE OF EVENTS

Only once have I met a couple who wanted to marry and had nothing in common. They had been referred by their therapist, who recommended they not marry. All I could find in common was that they both had master numbers (and not even the same ones). However, they wanted to marry, not to have someone attempt to talk them out of it. I concluded they really had a special mission to do here and needed each other. Because of their master numbers, I felt theirs to be a spiritual relationship and advised them to keep focusing on their love and not their differences.

In comparing two charts, the first thing I ask myself is what has brought these people together. To answer this, I compare EVERY-THING. I look for the same number to show up ANYWHERE, not particularly only in the same position in the chart. The more positions in which a number appears, the more connection there may be. Check and compare *every* point.

•Look at the Planes of Expression as this can be a solid foundation upon which to build, even with no other compatible numbers and without the numbers being on exactly the same plane.

•Look at the Pinnacles and Challenges. If they are identical the relationship may last only during the period of the similarity of the numbers.

•Check the Inclusion Table to see if it's an old karmic relationship. If the *same* amounts of the *same* number appear in the same positions, open your intuition to get a feel for the lives they may have shared, or similar strengths they may now have.

•Check the Personal Years; relationships beginning in a 9 personal year may just be for a few months to teach something about love, or may be the completion of some past lifetime. Encourage them to wait until the 1 year, or at least until October if they're planning marriage. (Although one of the "most alive" marriages I know was formalized during the summer of a "9" year for the husband.)

•There is a good connection when the Birthpath of one person is the Destiny of the other, and vice versa.

•A common connection is where the *first name* of one equals the Destiny of the other. Sound relationships are built by having the same goals, walking on the same path, learning the same lessons, or having the same Heart's Desire.

•Look at the Attainment and the Cycle of Wisdom. Will they share interests later in life? Some relationships are possible in later years that could never have worked earlier.

•2's and 6's are the numbers representing partnerships. Wherever they are found, i.e. the Pinnacles, Challenges, Personal Years, they are vibrations that represent times where there might be extra stress in relationships or the special blessings of deepening commitments. These problems are often their own issues and have nothing to do with their partner. People having more of these numbers have more focus on relationships.

•Women with a 1 Pinnacle or Challenge commonly need someone in their life who challenges them to take a greater stand in their life. Whoever is filling that role is doing them a loving favor!

•Always focus on the love more than the problems— problems come and go. Love is a special thing worth making adjustments for.

•Things commonly end when "9" is present. They may *change their form* and come back or be gone, leaving only the love remaining.

•Read "Conflicts with Other Numbers" from Section I.

•The *stress* found in a relationship is available by *subtracting* any of the numbers in important positions. For example, subtract 5 from 7 and the stress to be found is 2 = the need for greater patience with each other and more tact. (1 would represent the importance of a relationship of individuals, each strong in their own way.)

•*Never* attempt to talk someone out of a relationship based on their numbers. They are together for some reason—you don't have to know what it is. Assist them in having more harmony. Point out any areas of compatibility, or if you can't find them, admit it *is* challenging and look for 3's in the chart and emphasize the need to laugh and be playful together to help them over the difficult times.

The most effective counseling can be done by explaining one person to the other. No matter how much they might want to be someone else, they're themselves. Best is to accept what's there and find ways to bring in more humor and better communication as they expand and grow. Remember, they are together for that opportunity. While I think each number has a problem with the one next to it, I also think, with time, it turns into strengths. I would never tell two people they had a bad relationship. Use every opportunity to be positive; focus first on the strengths and then look into the problem areas. It seems to remove a lot of guilt to have their problem areas confirmed by an outside source like Numerology. This takes them completely out of the area of "should's" and "ought to's."

Many years ago, one of my first clients told me I'd presented her lots of information, but she didn't know what to do with it. That set me to thinking and gave me the focus necessary to lay out a chart and orient it toward what seemed valuable and pertinent. You, dear reader, plus my students and clients, have continually benefited from that remark. There is so much information available through Numerology...much more than presented here. I've distilled what is the most meaningful to me. As a 7, my question, even as a child, was "What is life about? Does it have a meaning?" I investigated religions, philosophies, even tried on existentialism. The study of Numerology has come close to answering these questions for me. It comforts me to think that life really has a purpose and meaning. Even if it's not so, and I'm all wrong, it won't make any difference; I've had lots of fun all these years thinking that I understood a little bit!

Throughout the book Amelia Earhart has been our example. She "disappeared" when I was a year old and was always a mysterious figure to me, and I know to many others. I enjoy using her name and birthday for examples as recognition of my admiration for her. So here's a little background on her, and then we'll chart out her full "game board" and do a relationship comparison with her huband.

Aviation and Amelia were young together. Amelia and her sister were the only children in the Earhart family. She grew up feeling women needed to live their lives with the freedom men enjoyed. She had a deep desire to "dare to live," and believed women should share with men, not surrender to them. In 1919, she pursued pre-medical studies. Later, one of her professors remarked, "Who knows what she would have discovered if she had chosen the research laboratory rather than aviation as a career?" Amelia learned flying from the first woman flight instructor, soloed at 24, and owned her own plane by 26. In 1922, she set her first record by climbing to an altitude mark of 14,000 feet. In 1927, Charles A. Lindburgh soloed from New York to Paris and captured everyone's imagination and heart. George Putnam, of G. P. Putnam's Sons Publishing Company, who persuaded Lindburgh to write the story of his flight, thought a woman's story of the same event would sell just as well. Looking around for a female with a flier's license and an extraordinary amount of courage, he came up with Amelia as the perfect candidate. Not only did she have writing skills, she resembled Lindburgh. In 1928, she became the first woman *passenger* to fly the Atlantic, and became an overnight sensation. They called her "Lady Lindy," a title that made her uncomfortable since she hadn't piloted it herself. "Putnam oozed confidence, dependability, love of freedom and adventure." He believed he could do or have anything if he desired it enough, and set out to have Amelia. She married him shortly after her father passed away in 1931, against the objections of her mother and many friends. Together, they got involved in many business and publicity schemes. "With Amelia's need for accomplishment and George's hunger for publicity, other challenges were inevitable." Five years after Lindburgh's feat, she became the first woman to fly solo across the Atlantic Ocean, experiencing terrible weather, wing icing, and fire from a leaking tank, to do it.

She became a valid heroine now, and numerous awards were bestowed upon her. Her feats of bravery continued in many races, setting countless "firsts" and winning great honors. In 1935, she became the first woman to solo fly Hawaii to California, Los Angeles to Mexico City, and Mexico City to New Jersey. Following this, she joined the faculty of Purdue University as visiting counselor for women students, and set out to be the first woman to fly around the world. This is where the intrigue enters the story. While most of the country assumed she was setting out on another "first," many think she was on an espionage mission for the United States. Her plane was outfitted with so many extras it was probably the U-2 of her day. When she took possession of it on her 38th birthday (July 24, 1936), she dubbed it her "Flying Laboratory." After many complications, she and the navigator, Fred Noonan, were finally off on May 20, 1937, and disappeared July 2, 1937. For more details on this fascinating tale, read *The Search for Amelia Earhart* by Fred Goerner (Doubleday and Company, Inc., 1966, and see Bibliography).

╳

In reading a chart, I like to start with the Birthday information as it presents a look at what was happening *when.* Even if the name is changed, birthdays stay the same, so it seems the "logical" place to start. Amelia's birthday was July 24, 1898, which reduces to 7, 6, 8 = 3. Taking note of the Cycle of Youth: 7. Her first Pinnacle: 4; and Challenge: 1; along with the deeper insight offered by the *Advanced Method* Pinnacle: 31; and Challenge: 17; we see the foundation laid during the first 33 years of Amelia's life was in great dedication to gaining wisdom of the unknown, blazing new trails, being disciplined and hard working, with an eye toward being creative and the innocence to try new things. Although her Birthpath is "3," it's composed of 5 + 7, which emphasize dedication from the 7 and love of freedom from the 5. 7 has a great drive for perfection and is brilliant at anything it sets its mind to, especially anything mysterious or perplexing. It loves spy missions and scientific research (remember her professor's remark?). Scanning the compound numbers, there are three 7's to be found from her Birthday numbers. Looking to her name, we see 7 is her Destiny number and the Heart's Desire of both "Amelia" and "Earhart" is 7. In the Simplified Version of Challenges, three out of four of them are 1's, her Attainment number is 1, plus she has five 1's in the Inclusion Table. That all translates into her approach to life being a courageous one. Past life experiences had imbued her with great inner strength, and she was challenging herself to develop and demonstrate more this time around.

Around 28, she cycled to her birthday 24 = 6 on the Cycle of Maturity, which assisted her into marrying a few years later.

3 Birthpath: 3 has been called the "fair-haired number of Numerology," and she was fair. Creative? Optimistic? Innocent? Certainly! Only someone looking at the positive side of life could have taken the risks she took. She certainly displayed a lot of those qualities plus she was also a writer and designer of women's clothes.

In 1932 she entered her new Pinnacle: 5 (Advanced Method: 50); and Challenge: 2. The Challenge was partnerships, marriage, getting along diplomatically with all the people in the new social circles, and serving as visiting counselor. 2 represents feminine energies: her position was counselor to women students, and she was designing "recklessly gay" sports clothes for women. The Pinnacle was expansion, new experiences, freedom, travel, progressive ideas, risk-taking, and adventuring. This was the time she started setting so many records.

Moving over to her name: Amelia = 5, with a first vowel A for extra courage. Her Heart's Desire is 4 (31), coupled with 4 on the Physical Plane of Expression, indicating tenacity, great discipline, ability to organize and follow through with anything that fascinated her. Probably without the 6 from her Birthday and 6 on the Mental Plane she might never have married. With all those 1's, she certainly knew she didn't "have" to do anything simply because it was expected. The 6's also indicate a strong desire to be of service.

Planes of Expression: Mental, 6, indicates one who likes to be recognized and appreciated for their accomplishments, yet her 7's indicate one who likes to stay out of the public eye—she did astonishing things alone in the sky that rewarded her with fame when she returned to earth. Some of her motivation starts to emerge. Mental, 6, patriotic, responsible, devoted to family, service, willing to put needs of others ahead of her own desires. Also, calm in emergencies. She handled her problems by thinking them out and being responsible.

Physical, 4, indicates great solidness, stamina, and ability to overcome all obstacles; good organizational skills, and well-suited to handle stress.

Emotion, 2. This could indicate someone shy and insecure, yet her other numbers prevented her from allowing her sensitivity to surface. It reveals great intuitive abilities.

Intuition, 5. This is another position that contributed to her love of freedom; from it we can assume she was very *in tune* with her inner radar and sonar system.

The Inclusion Table is highest in 1's—the courage she displayed, lots of masculine energy, favored position for a writer. Next highest are 9's—love for beauty, drama, the intensity of life, and humanitarian concerns. Low in 5's—out-of-balance desire for freedom; missing 6's—not real accomplished in handling the responsibilities of home and family.

Looking at her Table of Events: 1932 was a huge shift for her in almost every area. It was her 1 Personal Year, plus there was a change in her letters: E to L on the first line, bringing more creativity; and R to T on the third, bringing more focus on partnerships; with R on the middle line to intensify things and make them more dramatic and worldly. The Essence adds to 14 = 1 of inner strength, 4 of determination, totaling 5, freedom.

Reviewing her past: "A" commonly denotes a one-year period of changes; when she soloed in 1921, there was one present. It was also her "8" personal year, a time to take more control of her life. When she found her identity as a flier and bought her biplane in 1922, there were two present. It was a "9" Personal Year and time to complete and move on to bigger things. One "A" was present in 1924, the year her parents divorced, it was her "2" Personal Year of partnerships coming together or splitting apart, and the Essence was "14" which reduces to "5"—change. Her Dad died in her "9" Year, of completions, and she married then. Marriage at this time requires lots of letting go of personal concerns and asks total acceptance and love to allow it to work well. George was in a "3" Personal Year, the number of her Birthpath.

So let's compare their charts.

From what I've heard, read, and his 8 Heart and "8" First Challenge, I doubted this to be a love relationship. Asking myself, "What has brought these two people together," although I noticed his first name equals her Birthpath, I still wondered if this was a marriage of advantages. George offered financial support and someone to be an authority for her to rely on. She would offer him excitement, fame, and additional fortune. All of this certainly was part of the attraction. Yet, comparing their Planes of Expression, there is a good basis for solid communication that no outsider could perceive. He has 6's on both the Physical and Intuitive Planes—she on the Mental, which means he could easily tune into her thoughts and understand her. This is further corroborated by his 2 on the Mental and her 2 on the Emotional. Also notice they both had 4's, which meant they could plan and organize together. This is also a good example of the importance first Pinnacles and Challenges have in molding lives. The foundation they laid in his life were for cooperation and pursuit of the unknown.

Comparing their Inclusion Tables shows them having the same amount of 2's and 4's, from which we can guess that lifetimes past had been spent together, perhaps married, perhaps as builders. By subtracting two 5's from his total of 5's we see his highest amount is 7's. This is Amelia's Destiny number, and could infer he'd spent lifetimes developing faith and trust. This is an interesting connection, especially as 7 is so commonly missing in others' charts. His strongest point was what she was here in life demonstrating. This is a good example of the intricacies of relationships. Also notice the new compatibility when she became Amelia Earhart Putnam.

Another connection is the 4 in her heart and the 8 in his. Very compatible numbers. Looking for the *stresses* from Birthpaths, 4 − 3 = 1; Heart's Desires, 8 − 4 = 4; Destinies, 9 − 7 = 2. The stresses came with her need to be an individual; the need for organizaiton and tenacity, and the need for cooperation and tact.

Just by being able to guess about their lifestyles, it's easy to imagine this to be very valid.

From a quick glance at his Table of Events: anyone starting life with a G and 2 P's (all 7's) would be very "unusual," perhaps towards strange, certainly misunderstood. No one ever understood him, and he never knew why.

I've not mentioned his Master Numbers, while they certainly pushed him into being a world-wide figure, yet I have a theory that Master Numbers have greater importance in our lives *these* days than at any time in the past.

She disappeared in 1937; it was her 6 Personal Year and his 9. Look at their Pinnacles and Challenges that follow this time, and draw your own conclusions....

And *really,* draw your own conclusions is the best advice I can give you. I can *teach* you how Numerology works, I can *define, diagram* and *explain,* but only YOU can practice until you know what you're doing. Only *you* can risk feeling foolish and dare to say what comes into your mind—which is allowing your inner knower to step forward (perhaps your inner Numerologist). About 15 years ago, I bought a game entitled "Numerology"—half-price, at a going-out-of-business sale. If someone had told me that one day I'd know enough Numerology to write a book, they might have seemed pretty ridiculous. Fortunately, no one did, and I just bumbled along with it as a hobby for many years. By the time I became acquainted with Dr. Juno Jordan, I met her as an associate. We had a great afternoon visit, and she said she felt happy to leave Numerology in the hands of people like me. Clearly, the highest praise I could have received.

Perhaps you can guess that I was the one in the Fairy Tale who looked at numbers with a new eye and said, "Hmmmm, I think I'll dig around and find out what I can about these strange little symbols." And clearly, it has been the most amazing search of my life. It has led me into a career I love, most of my clients have become dear friends, and my understanding of Numerology has assisted many people to feel more directed, balanced, and joyful about their lives. It has opened the door to countless adventures, and generally made my "5's and 7's" very happy.

The spells witches put out are having less influence on our lives all the time. Meanwhile, people everywhere are enjoying the benefits of accepting and understanding themselves a little better, and are seeing the importance of "walking a mile in someone else's moccasins." Whoever inhabits your personal world — your children, friends, lovers, parents, students, clients, or bosses — reap the benefits of your added enlightenment. I want to create a world where we all work together in harmony and cooperation, and writing this book was the best way I knew to help. God bless us, every one.

So, we'll end with the beautiful words of Julia Seton Sears: "Man does not go far in the search after secrets of himself and understanding of the world in which he lives before he finds that we are all named, numbered, chorded, colored, and placed in a perfect universal and personal plan."

I will be happy to answer any questions, as my time permits.

ℵ

Bibliography

Balliett, Mrs. L. Dow. *The Philosophy of Numbers*. Atlantic City, NJ: 1908. (Note: Reprints of all of Mrs. Ballietts's books available through Health Research, 70 Lafayette Street, Mokelumne Hill, CA 95245.)

_____. *Nature's Symphony*. Atlantic City, NJ: 1911.

Carey, Kenneth. *The Starseed Transmission. Kenneth Carey, Star Route, Box 70, Mt. View, MO 65548, 1982.*

d'Olivet, Fabre. *Golden Verses of Pythagoras*. Published in French, 1813. Reprinted New York: Samuel Weiser, Inc., 1975.

Goerner, Fred. *The Search for Amelia Earhart*. New York: Doubleday and Company, Inc., 1966.

Henninger, S. K., Jr. *Touches of Sweet Harmony*. The Hunnington Library, San Marino, CA., 1974.

Jordan, Juno. *Numerology, The Romance in Your Name*. DeVorss & Co., Publishers, Santa Barbara, CA., 1975.

Lawlor, Robert. *Sacred Geometry, Philosophy and Practice*. New York: Crossroads Publications, 1982.

Michell, John. *City of Revelation*. New York: Ballantine Books, 1972.

Pellegreno, Ann H. *World Flight, The Earhart Trail*. The Iowa State University Press, 1971.

Shure, Edouard. *Pythagoras*. London: Wm. Rider & Son, Ltd., 1923.

Taylor, Thomas (trans.), *Iamblichus' Life of Pythagoras*. Rochester, VT: Inner Traditions, International, 1986.

THE NEW AGE AFFIRMATION CALENDAR

This inspiring, day-by-day calendar features one uplifting affirmation for each day of the year. Special affirmations are geared to holidays. reflecting the positive spirit of each event. Calendar pages include: • an affirmation at the top • the day, week, and year in striking, large type • a small inset calendar that shows the month at a glance • holiday notations • plenty of space for taking notes or jotting down reminders. *The New Age Affirmation Calendar* is an ideal gift and the perfect means for overcoming doubts and worries, and for enhancing self-esteem, goals, and serenity every day of the year.

$8.95, Daily calendar, ISBN 0-944132-06-5
Calendar, 365pp, 4½ x 5¼

Skidmore-Roth Publishing

"I am enjoying every aspect of my life"

NEW AGE AFFIRMATION CALENDAR

BY ELIZABETH MOORE

Warm Logic
— The —
Art of Intuitive
— Lifestyle —
A guide for your personal, ethical & spiritual fulfillment

Louis Wynne, Ph.D.
Carolyn S. Klintworth, M.A.

Respecting, expressing, and acting on our feelings is the focus of this guide to a balanced, more intuitive way of living.

WARM LOGIC

The Art of the Intuitive Lifestyle
Louis Wynne, Ph.D.
and Carolyn S. Klintworth, M.A.

Warm Logic is about feelings—caring, compassion, intimacy, joy, and fulfillment, as well as confusion, anguish, and despair—and what we can and must do to understand and express our feelings. By doing this, say the authors, we can harness our feelings and realign our lives in greater harmony with nature. "Warm logic," write Wynne and Klintworth, "is the wisdom of nature manifesting itself as wordless guidance." The book tells how to hear and heed that guidance, and counter the frustration and tension that can mount when our inituitive, emotional selves are stymied by the expectations we feel others have of us.

Louise Wynne, Ph.D. lives in Albuquerque, NM.
Carolyn S. Klintworth, M.A. lives in Santa Fe, NM.

April, $12.95, Trade paper, ISBN 0-944132-11-1
New Age/Self-Help, 250pp, 6 x 9

Skidmore-Roth Publishing